MW01108097

Expression
of
Appreciation

I wish to thank all of my chocolate lover friends who have contributed to this cookbook by donating cherished recipes and those who have encouraged me to publish this cookbook.

I wish to convey my sincere appreciation to all those who have helped in any way with the compiling and selling of this cookbook or otherwise.

About Author

A cookbook of carefully selected recipes by Jean Foster, a Southerner whose love for cooking and good food has led her to a lifetime search of naturally good recipes and fine kitchen ware. Former owner of a gift-gourmet cookware store, she has spent much time and effort finding beautiful and worthy cooking accessories and naturally good recipes (especially chocolate).

Just Make Mine Chocolate, Please

Just make mine chocolate, please,
If it's dessert,
Just make mine chocolate, please.
A shake, that's o.k.
Just make mine chocolate, please.
Whatever is served, I'll just love.
Just make mine chocolate, please.

About Chocolate

Such a delicious delightful sweet treat. It comes from an evergreen tree of the genus Theobroma. It is made from the beans of the cacao and used as a flavoring and an ingredient in beverages and other confectionary.

Chocolate was brought to Europe by the Spaniards who learned of its use from the Mexicans at the time of the invasion by Cortes in 1519. It was introduced in England about 1657.

In the U.S., chocolate was first made in Milton Lower Mills, near Dorchester, Massachusetts, in 1765. In recent years the U.S. has consumed almost one half of the world's production of chocolate. More than 600,000,000 pounds annually!

Chocolate comes in powder, syrup and bars. Carob is a chocolate substitute and white chocolate contains no chocolate at all.

TABLE OF CONTENTS

FAVORITE RECIPES
FROM MY COOKBOOK

Recipe Name	Page Number

CAKES, CUPCAKES, FILLINGS, AND FROSTINGS

MILKY WAY CAKE

This old-time Southern favorite tastes even better the next day. It freezes well, too.

1½ c. plus 2 Tbsp. butter
1 c. finely chopped pecans (4 oz.)
14 oz. Milky Way bars (about 6½ individual size), cut up
2½ c. all-purpose flour
¾ tsp. baking soda

¼ tsp. salt
1½ c. granulated sugar
4 large eggs
1 tsp. vanilla
1¼ c. buttermilk

Heat oven to 325°. Grease a 10 inch fluted tube pan with the 2 tablespoons butter. Add chopped nuts; tilt and rotate pan to cover bottom and sides. Leave any loose nuts in bottom of pan. Heat candy bars and ½ cup butter in a heavy saucepan over low heat, stirring often until melted and smooth. Remove from heat; cool slightly. Mix flour, baking soda, and salt. In a large bowl, beat remaining 1 cup butter and the sugar with electric mixer until fluffy. Add eggs one at a time, beating well after each addition. Beat in vanilla and candy mixture. Add flour mixture alternately with buttermilk until well blended. Scrape into prepared pan. Bake about 1 hour or until pick inserted in center comes out clean. Cool in pan on rack 30 minutes. Invert on rack; remove pan and cool completely. Makes 12 servings.

CHOCOLATE-ALMOND CAKE WITH CHERRY FILLING

Another chocolate favorite cake.

4 (1 oz.) sq. semi-sweet chocolate
2 (8 oz.) cans almond paste
1 c. sugar
1 egg
⅔ c. butter, softened

4 eggs
2 tsp. vanilla extract
1½ tsp. almond extract
2 c. cake flour, sifted

Cherry Filling:

¼ c. cherry or strawberry preserves
1 c. sifted confectioners sugar

1 Tbsp. brandy or milk
1 tsp. almond extract

Place chocolate in top of double boiler; bring water to a boil. Reduce heat, and cook until chocolate melts. Cool slightly.

Crumble 1 can almond paste into a large mixing bowl. Add 1 cup sugar and 1 egg; beat at medium speed of an electric mixer until well blended. Add butter and beat until blended. Add 4 eggs, one at a time, beating well after each addition. Beat in melted chocolate, vanilla, and 1½ teaspoons almond extract. Add flour, a little at a time, beating at low speed just until blended.

Pour batter into 2 greased and floured 9 inch round cake pans; bake at 325° for 35 minutes or until a wooden pick inserted in center comes out clean. Cool cake in pans 10 minutes on a wire rack; remove from pans and cool completely.

Place one layer on a serving plate; place waxed paper strips under edge of cake, covering plate. Spread half of Cherry Filling on cake layer, and top with second cake layer. Melt cherry preserves; press through a fine-meshed sieve to remove lumps of fruit. Brush sieved preserves on sides of cake. Spoon remaining Cherry Filling on top of cake, spreading just to edge.

Combine remaining can of almond paste, confectioners sugar, brandy, and 1 teaspoon almond extract in a large mixing bowl; mix at low to medium speed until crumbly. Knead until well blended (mixture will be soft and pliable). Roll out almond paste mixture on a piece of waxed paper into a strip 28 inches long and 3 inches wide, trimming to make strip even. Using waxed paper to help lift and guide almond paste strip, wind strip around side of cake, pressing edges firmly together to adhere. Lightly press strip onto side of cake. Cut ½ inch slits at ½ inch intervals around top edge of almond paste strip; gently bend alternating "fingers" back and forth to create a herringbone effect. If a "finger" breaks off from cake, moisten the almond paste lightly with water, and gently press back onto cake. Cover until serving time. Serves 12.

Cherry Filling:

2 (16½ oz.) cans pitted tart cherries (undrained)

¼ c. brandy
3 Tbsp. cornstarch

Drain cherries, reserving 1⅓ cups liquid. Set cherries aside. Combine reserved cherry liquid, brandy, and cornstarch in a small saucepan, stirring until smooth. Cook over medium heat, stirring occasionally, until mixture thickens. Cool slightly. Stir in cherries; cool to room temperature. Makes 3 cups.

GERMAN BLACK FOREST CHERRY CAKE

A rich and lovely cake. Perfect for a special company dinner.

½ lb. fresh dark sweet cherries, pitted or 1 c. canned dark sweet cherries, drained and pitted
8 Tbsp. Kirschwasser
½ c. sifted cake flour
½ c. sifted cocoa
6 eggs, separated
1½ c. granulated sugar

1 tsp. vanilla
½ tsp. salt
½ tsp. cream of tartar
5½ Tbsp. butter, clarified
Cocoa and butter (for pan)
2 c. heavy cream
½ c. confectioners sugar
Semi-sweet chocolate curls

Combine cherries and 2 tablespoons of the Kirschwasser in small saucepan and let stand while preparing cake.

Sift together flour and cocoa. Beat egg yolks in small bowl with electric mixer on high speed until very thick and lemon colored, about 5 minutes. Add ½ cup of the granulated sugar, vanilla, and salt. Beat until sugar is dissolved and mixture forms a ribbon when beater is lifted, 2 to 3 minutes.

Wash and dry beaters thoroughly. Beat egg whites and cream of tartar in large mixer bowl at high speed until foamy, then gradually beat in ½ cup of granulated sugar. Beat until stiff peaks form and sugar is dissolved. Gently fold dry mixture into yolk mixture. Fold 2 large spoonfuls of egg whites into yolk mixture. Pour yolk mixture over remaining whites and gently fold together just until blended. Gently fold in butter, about 2 tablespoons at a time. Divide batter evenly between 2 buttered and cocoa-dusted 8 inch round cake pans. Bake in preheated 350°F. oven until center of cake springs back when lightly touched, 25 to 30 minutes. Cool cakes 5 minutes; carefully remove from pans and cool on wire racks.

Add 2 tablespoons water to cherries in saucepan. Heat to simmering over medium low heat. Reduce heat to low and simmer until cherries are tender, about 5 minutes. Drain, reserving liquid. Heat 2 tablespoons of the liquid and remaining ½ cup granulated sugar to simmering in small saucepan over medium low heat. Simmer until very syrupy, about 3 minutes. Remove saucepan from heat and stir in 4 table-spoons Kirschwasser.

Cut cake layers in half horizontally to make 4 thin layers. Drizzle syrup mixture evenly over cut sides of each layer, spreading with spatula to cover evenly.

Whip cream in medium bowl at high speed until soft peaks form, then add confectioners sugar and remaining 2 tablespoons Kirschwasser. Continue beating until soft peaks are formed.

Place 1 cake layer, cut side up, on serving plate. Spread with scant ¾ cup whipped cream. Top with second cake layer, cut side down; spread with scant ¾ cup whipped cream. Reserve 6 cherries for garnish and arrange remaining cherries over whipped cream on cake layers. Top with third cake layer, cut side up, and spread with scant ¾ cup whipped cream. Top with finally cake layer, cut side down. Frost top and sides of cake with remaining whipped cream. Garnish with reserved cherries and chocolate curls. Refrigerate until serving time. Cut into wedges to serve. Serves 12.

CHOCOLATE VELVET CAKE

Makes a very rich one layer chocolate cake.

1 (4 oz.) pkg. sweet chocolate,
  broken in pieces
6 Tbsp. butter
3 Tbsp. all-purpose flour

3 eggs, separated
4 Tbsp. sugar
Chocolate Glaze

Melt chocolate and butter in saucepan over very low heat, stirring constantly, until smooth. Remove from heat; stir in flour. Blend in egg yolks, one at a time.

Beat egg whites until foamy throughout. Gradually beat in sugar; continue beating until soft peaks will form. Gently fold chocolate mixture into egg whites, blending thoroughly.

Pour into greased and floured 8 inch layer pan. Bake at 350° for about 20 minutes or until cake tester inserted in center comes out clean. Cool in pan 10 minutes (cake will settle slightly). Finish cooling, upside-down, on rack. Spread top and sides with Chocolate Glaze. Garnish as desired.

Chocolate Glaze: Melt 1 (4 ounce) package sweet chocolate, in pieces, and 3 tablespoons water over low heat, stirring constantly. Remove from heat; stir in 3 tablespoons butter. Cool to thicken in necessary. Serves 6.

VELVETY CREAM CHOCOLATE CAKE

A wonderful party perfect cake.

Cake Layers:

½ c. sifted all-purpose flour	¼ tsp. salt
¼ c. unsweetened cocoa powder	3 eggs
¼ tsp. ground cinnamon	⅔ c. sugar

Chocolate Creme:

1 env. unflavored gelatin	¼ c. water
3 Tbsp. unsweetened cocoa powder	1 c. cold milk
1 Tbsp. instant coffee	2 egg whites
Dash of ground cinnamon	3 Tbsp. sugar

Yogurt Topping:

1 env. unflavored gelatin	¾ c. plain yogurt
¼ c. water	4 to 6 large strawberries, quartered
1 egg white	Fresh mint leaves for garnish
1 Tbsp. sugar	(optional)
½ tsp. vanilla	

1. Prepare Cake Layer: Grease two 8 inch round cake pans; line bottoms with wax paper; grease paper. Preheat oven to 350°.

2. Sift together flour, cocoa, cinnamon, and salt onto piece of wax paper.

3. Beat eggs in small bowl until foamy. Gradually beat in sugar until thick and fluffy. Fold in flour mixture. Spoon into prepared pans, dividing evenly.

4. Bake in preheated moderate oven (350°) for 20 minutes or until tops spring back when lightly pressed with fingertip. Cool in pans on wire racks, 10 minutes. Loosen edges; invert cakes on racks. Cool completely. Place one layer on serving platter. Cover; set aside. Wrap and freeze the second layer for another use.

5. Prepare Chocolate Creme: Combine gelatin, cocoa powder, instant coffee, cinnamon, and water in cup. Stir until gelatin is softened. Place cup in hot water; stir to dissolve gelatin.

6. Combine cold milk and gelatin-cocoa mixture in small bowl. Chill until consistency of unbeaten egg whites.

7. Beat 2 egg whites in bowl until foamy. Gradually beat in sugar until soft peaks form. Fold chilled cocoa mixture into beaten whites until no white streaks remain. Pour into 1 quart metal mold or bowl, 6 to 7½ inches in diameter. Shake gently to remove large bubbles. Refrigerate several hours or overnight until firm.

8. To unmold, loosen edges of gelatin; quickly dip in warm water. Invert over cake layer; shake to loosen and carefully remove mold. Refrigerate until surface of mold has set again.

9. To prepare Yogurt Topping: Sprinkle gelatin over the water in small cup; let stand 5 minutes to soften. Set cup in hot water; stir to dissolve gelatin. Cool slightly.

10. Beat egg white in small bowl until foamy. Gradually beat in sugar until meringue forms soft peaks. Fold gelatin mixture and vanilla into yogurt in medium size bowl. Fold in beaten white. Spoon Yogurt Topping into pastry bag fitted with large star tip. Pipe up and down over side of mold, but leaving top sides of mold uncovered. Pipe topping on top of mold in small swirl. Garnish side and top with strawberries. Garnish each strawberry with fresh mint leaves, if you wish. Serves 10.

ROYAL CHOCOLATE CAKE

Another fine party cake with a fruit filling.

Grease and flour two 9 x 1½ inch round baking pans. Combine 2 cups all-purpose flour, 1 teaspoon each baking powder and soda, and ½ teaspoon salt. Beat ½ cup butter for 30 seconds. Add 1½ cups granulated sugar and 1 teaspoon vanilla; beat well. Add 2 eggs, beating 1 minute after each. Blend in 2 squares unsweetened chocolate, melted. Add dry ingredients and 1 cup water alternately to beaten mixture; beat well. Turn into pans. Bake in 350° oven for 30 to 35 minutes. Cool 10 minutes. Remove. Cool. Spread filling between layers. Frost. Serves 12.

Filling: Combine ¾ cup water, ½ cup light raisins, ½ cup chopped dates, ¼ cup granulated sugar, 2 tablespoons chopped maraschino cherries, 1 tablespoon chopped candied ginger, and 1 tablespoon cornstarch. Cook till bubbly. Stir in 1 teaspoon lemon juice. Makes about 2 cups.

Frosting: Beat ⅓ cup butter till fluffy. Beat in ¾ cup sifted confectioners sugar, 1 egg, and 1 teaspoon vanilla. Add ¾ cup sifted confectioners sugar; beat smooth. Beat in 2 squares unsweetened chocolate, melted, till fluffy. Makes about 2 cups.

SOUR CREAM CHOCOLATE CAKE

The sour cream gives this cake a different texture.

2¼ c. sifted all-purpose flour
1 tsp. baking powder
1 c. boiling water
½ c. (1 stick) butter
3 sq. unsweetened chocolate
2 c. sugar

1 tsp. vanilla
2 eggs, separated
½ c. dairy sour cream
1 tsp. baking soda
Chocolate Frosting (recipe follows)

1. Preheat oven to moderate (350°). Grease bottom and side of a 10 inch springform pan; dust lightly with flour. Tap out any excess.

2. Sift flour and baking powder onto wax paper.

3. Pour boiling water over butter and chocolate in a large bowl; let stand 5 minutes until melted; stir to blend. Stir in sugar and vanilla. Beat in egg yolks, one at a time, blending thoroughly.

4. Combine sour cream and baking soda in a bowl; beat into chocolate mixture. Stir in flour mixture, blending thoroughly.

5. Beat egg whites in a small bowl with electric mixer until soft peaks form. Stir a little of the beaten egg whites into batter to lighten. Fold remaining egg whites into chocolate mixture until no streaks of white remain. Pour into prepared pan.

6. Bake in preheated moderate oven (350°) for 45 minutes or until a small knife inserted near center comes out clean. Cool cake in pan on wire rack 10 minutes; loosen spring from side. Remove side of pan; cool cake completely. Frost with Chocolate Frosting. Serves 12.

Chocolate Frosting:

¾ c. semi-sweet chocolate pieces (from a 6 oz. pkg.)
6 Tbsp. heavy cream

2 Tbsp. butter
1 tsp. vanilla
1¼ c. confectioners sugar

1. Combine chocolate, heavy cream, butter, vanilla, and sugar in a medium size saucepan.

2. Heat slowly, stirring constantly, until butter and chocolate have melted. Remove from heat; beat until mixture thickens slightly, but is still runny. Cool slightly. Frost Chocolate Cake. (Frosting is soft and runny, but firms up on cake.) Makes enough to frost one 10 inch cake.

DISAPPEARING CAKE

A rich, moist, and chocolatey cake that will disappear fast!

¼ c. butter
¼ c. shortening
2 c. sugar
1 tsp. vanilla
2 eggs
¾ c. cocoa

1¾ c. unsifted all-purpose flour
¾ tsp. baking powder
¾ tsp. baking soda
⅛ tsp. salt
1¾ c. milk

Generously grease and flour two 9 inch round cake pans. Cream butter, shortening, sugar, and vanilla until fluffy; blend in eggs. Combine cocoa, flour, baking powder, baking soda, and salt in bowl; add alternately with milk to batter. Blend well. Pour into pans; bake at 350° for 30 to 35 minutes or until cake tester inserted in center comes out clean. Cool 10 minutes; remove from pans. Frost with your favorite frosting recipe. Serves 12.

PIE-PAN FUDGE CAKE

This super-rich cake is marvelous as a gift. It's baked in a foil pan that's easy to wrap and transport.

6 eggs, separated
½ c. butter, softened
¾ c. sugar
1 Tbsp. vanilla

6 (1 oz.) sq. semi-sweet chocolate, melted and cooled
½ c. flour
¼ c. chopped nuts (optional)

In small bowl of mixer, beat egg whites until stiff; set aside. With same beaters in large bowl of mixer, cream butter, sugar, and vanilla until light. Beat in all the chocolate, then the egg yolks in three portions until well blended. Stir in flour. Fold in egg whites lightly but thoroughly. Pour into 2 greased 9 inch foil pie pans. Sprinkle with nuts. Bake in preheated 300° oven for 45 minutes or until pick inserted in center comes out clean. Cool in pan on rack. Store airtight in cool, dry place. Keeps about 3 weeks. Serve in slender wedges. Serves 16.

CHOCOLATE-ZUCCHINI CAKE

A deliciously different chocolate cake!

½ c. plus 1 Tbsp. butter, softened
2 c. sugar
3 (1 oz.) sq. unsweetened
  chocolate, melted and cooled
3 eggs
½ c. milk
2 tsp. grated orange rind
2 tsp. vanilla
2 c. coarsely grated unpeeled
  zucchini

2½ c. all-purpose flour
2½ tsp. baking soda
½ tsp. salt
1 tsp. ground cinnamon
2 Tbsp. confectioners sugar
½ tsp. ground cinnamon
Whole fresh strawberries (optional)

Cream butter; gradually add 2 cups sugar, beating until light and fluffy. Beat in chocolate. Add eggs, one at a time, beating well after each addition. Beat in next 4 ingredients.

Combine flour, baking powder, soda, salt, and 1 teaspoon cinnamon; add to creamed mixture, mixing well. Pour batter into a greased and floured 10 inch Bundt pan. Bake at 350° for 1 hour and 5 minutes or until a wooden pick inserted in center comes out clean. Cool in pan for 10 to 15 minutes; remove from pan and place on a wire rack.

Combine confectioners sugar and ½ teaspoon cinnamon; sift over warm cake. Cool completely. Fill center of cake with strawberries if desired. Serves 12.

CHOCOLATE BEET CAKE

Another chocolate delicious cake with an unusual ingredient.

2 c. all-purpose flour
2 tsp. baking powder
½ tsp. salt
⅓ c. cocoa
3 eggs
1 c. sugar
1 c. cooked grated beets

½ c. corn oil
¼ c. orange juice
2 tsp. grated orange rind
1 tsp. vanilla
1 (6 oz.) pkg. semi-sweet chocolate
  morsels
Confectioners sugar (optional)

Combine flour, baking powder, salt, and cocoa; set aside. Combine eggs and sugar in a large mixing bowl; mix well. Add beets, oil, orange juice, and orange rind to sugar mixture; beat well. Stir in flour mixture and vanilla, mixing well. Stir in chocolate morsels.

Pour into a greased 9 inch square baking pan. Bake at 350° for 40 minutes or until cake tests done. Let cool 10 minutes in pan. Remove from pan and cool completely on wire rack. Sprinkle with confectioners sugar if desired. Makes 16 servings.

DEEP, DARK CHOCOLATE CAKE

Mixes in 5 minutes.

1¾ c. unsifted all-purpose flour
2 c. sugar
¾ c. cocoa
1½ tsp. baking soda
1½ tsp. baking powder
1 tsp. salt

2 eggs
1 c. milk
½ c. vegetable oil
2 tsp. vanilla
1 c. boiling water

Combine dry ingredients in large mixer bowl. Add eggs, milk, oil, and vanilla. Beat 2 minutes at medium speed. Stir in boiling water (batter will be thin). Pour into greased and floured 13x9x2 inch pan. Bake at 350° for 35 to 40 minutes or until cake tester inserted in center comes clean. Cool. Serves 12. Frost with One-Bowl Buttercream Frosting.

One-Bowl Buttercream Frosting:

6 Tbsp. butter, softened
Cocoa (⅓ c. for light flavor, ½ c. for medium flavor, ¾ c. for dark flavor)

2⅔ c. unsifted confectioners sugar

Cream butter in small mixer bowl. Add cocoa and confectioners sugar alternately with milk; beat to spreading consistency (additional tablespoon milk may be needed). Blend in vanilla. Makes about 2 cups frosting.

TRIANON

This is a very dense cake, but don't be surprised if, after unmolding, the sides cave in slightly and it crumbles a bit on top. Best to wait a day before slicing.

2 c. (12 oz.) semi-sweet chocolate chips
1¼ c. unsalted butter, cut in pieces
1 c. granulated sugar
6 large or 5 extra large eggs, yolks and white separated
Pinch of salt

1 c. minus 2 Tbsp. all-purpose flour, or 1 c. cake flour
Unsweetened whipped cream (optional)
Raspberry sauce (made by pureeing 10 oz. pkg. frozen raspberries in blender; optional)

Place rack in lower third of oven. Heat oven to 325°. Generously grease an 8 cup loaf pan (9¼ x 5¼ x 2¾ inch and 10¼ x 3⅝ x 2⅝ inch pans are readily available). Line bottom with waxed paper and grease paper. Put chocolate and butter in a heavy 1½ to 2 quart saucepan. Stir over medium low heat until mixture is melted and smooth. Add sugar; continue stirring 2 minutes until dissolved. Remove from heat; stir in yolks, one at a time, until incorporated. In a large bowl, beat egg whites and salt with electric mixer until firm shiny peaks form when beaters are lifted. Stir a large spoonful whites into chocolate mixture to lighten. Pour chocolate mixture over remaining whites. Sprinkle ⅓ flour at a time over top, folding in each addition until incorporated before adding more. Pour batter into prepared pan. Bake for 30 minutes. Check cake; if it's browning too much place a piece of foil on top. Continue baking 30 to 40 minutes until top is crusty and cake doesn't wiggle when pan is moved. Turn off oven; let cake set in oven with door closed 1 hour. Remove to cooling rack. Let cool completely in pan, 2 to 3 hours. Don't refrigerate to speed up cooling - you'll never get cake out of pan. When cool, loosen sides with small knife. Place cookie sheet on cake; invert. Lift off pan. Cake will be very fragile. Wrap in plastic wrap, then in foil. Slice and serve plain or with whipped cream and raspberry sauce. (Cake will be dry around the sides and dark and moist in middle.) Serves 12.

CHOCOLATE-PEANUT BUTTER CAKE

Two addictive ingredients make this a very delicious cake!

3¼ c. all-purpose flour
2¼ c. sugar
1 Tbsp. plus 1 tsp. baking powder
½ tsp. salt
½ c. butter, softened
½ c. creamy peanut butter
1½ c. milk
3 eggs

1⅓ c. finely chopped unsalted roasted peanuts
Chocolate-Peanut Butter Frosting
1 (6 oz.) pkg. semi-sweet chocolate morsels
2 to 4 Tbsp. chopped unsalted roasted peanuts

Combine first 4 ingredients in a large mixing bowl; mix well. Add butter, peanut butter, and milk; beat 2 minutes on medium speed of electric mixer. Add eggs; beat 2 minutes on medium speed. Fold in 1⅓ cups chopped peanuts.

Pour batter into 3 greased and floured 9 inch cake pans. Bake at 350° for 25 to 30 minutes or until a wooden pick inserted in center comes out clean (do not overbake). Cool in pans 10 minutes; remove layers from pans and cool completely.

Spread Chocolate-Peanut Butter Frosting between layers and on top and sides of cake; chill 1 hour or until firm.

Melt chocolate morsels in top of a double boiler over hot water. Drizzle around top edge and down sides of cake. Sprinkle 2 to 4 tablespoons chopped peanuts on top. Chill until ready to serve. Makes one 3 layer cake.

Chocolate-Peanut Butter Frosting:

1 (6 oz.) pkg. semi-sweet chocolate morsels
½ c. butter, softened

½ c. sifted confectioners sugar
1⅓ c. creamy peanut butter

Melt chocolate morsels in top of a double boiler over hot water; set aside. Combine remaining ingredients in a small mixing bowl; beat at medium speed of electric mixer until smooth. Add melted chocolate to peanut butter mixture; beat until smooth. Chill 15 minutes or until spreading consistency. Enough frosting for one 3 layer cake.

BLACKBOTTOM CUPCAKES

Arrange on a pretty plate and serve at tea time.

1½ c. all-purpose flour
1⅓ c. sugar
¼ c. unsweetened cocoa powder
1 tsp. baking soda
½ tsp. salt
1 c. water
5 Tbsp. vegetable oil

1 Tbsp. cider vinegar
1 tsp. vanilla
1 (8 oz.) pkg. cream cheese (room
   temperature)
1 egg
6 oz. semi-sweet chocolate chips

Preheat oven to 350°F. Grease muffin tins. Mix flour, 1 cup sugar, cocoa powder, baking soda, and salt in large bowl. Make well in center. Blend water, oil, vinegar, and vanilla. Pour into well. Gradually incorporated flour into liquid, whisking until smooth. Spoon batter into prepared pans.

Beat cream cheese, remaining ⅓ cup sugar and egg in medium bowl with electric mixer. Stir in chocolate chips. Spoon over batter. Bake until tester inserted in centers comes out clean, about 25 minutes. Cool in tins on racks 10 minutes. Remove from tins and cool. Store in airtight containers. Makes 18.

CHOCOLATISSIMO

Indeed, a very rich chocolate cake.

10 (1 oz.) sq. semi-sweet chocolate,
   broken up, or 1⅔ c. semi-
   sweet chocolate pieces
1 tsp. instant coffee powder

1¼ c. unsalted butter
1¼ c. sugar
10 eggs, separated

Melt chocolate with coffee in top of double boiler or bowl set over hot, not boiling, water. Stir until smooth; cool. In very large bowl, cream butter and sugar. Add cooled chocolate; blend well. Add egg yolks one at a time, beating well after each addition; beat for a total of 15 minutes. In another bowl with clean beaters, beat egg whites until stiff but not dry. Fold into chocolate mixture. Measure and refrigerate ¼ the mixture. Pour remainder into greased (bottom only) 9 inch springform pan. Bake in preheated 350° oven for 50 minutes. Cool completely in pan on rack. (Cake will sink in the middle.) Spread reserved chocolate mixture over top. Cover; chill overnight. (If desired, garnish with confectioners sugar.) Serve in thin slices. Makes 12 servings.

GERMAN SWEET CHOCOLATE CAKE

Delicious and my favorite chocolate cake!

1 (4 oz.) pkg. German's sweet
   chocolate
2⅓ c. sifted cake flour
1½ c. sugar
1 tsp. baking soda
½ tsp. baking powder

½ tsp. salt
⅔ c. butter
1 c. buttermilk
1 tsp. vanilla
2 eggs
Coconut-Pecan Filling and Frosting

Melt chocolate over very low heat; cool. Sift flour with sugar, soda, baking powder, and salt. Stir butter in mixer bowl to soften. Add flour mixture, ¾ cup of the buttermilk, and the vanilla. Mix to dampen flour; beat 2 minutes at medium speed of electric mixer, scraping bowl occasionally. Add melted chocolate, eggs, and remaining buttermilk. *Beat 1 minute longer.* Pour batter into three 8 inch layer pans, lined on bottoms with paper. Bake at 350° for 30 to 35 minutes, or until cake tester inserted into centers comes out clean. Cool in pans for 15 minutes; remove from pans and cool on racks. Spread filling on layers and stack. Serves 12.

Coconut-Pecan Filling and Frosting:

1 c. evaporated milk	**1 tsp. vanilla**
1 c. sugar	**1⅓ c. (about) flaked coconut**
3 egg yolks, slightly beaten	**1 c. chopped pecans**
½ c. butter	

Combine milk, sugar, egg yolks, butter, and vanilla in saucepan. Cook and stir over medium heat until mixture thickens, about 12 minutes. Remove from heat. Add coconut and pecans. Cool until spreading consistency beating occasionally.

COCOA FUDGE CAKE

A very old chocolate cake recipe made with buttermilk powder.

1⅔ c. all-purpose flour	**6 Tbsp. buttermilk powder**
1½ c. sugar	**1½ c. water**
⅔ c. cocoa	**½ c. shortening**
1½ tsp. soda	**2 eggs**
1 tsp. salt	**1 tsp. vanilla**

Have ingredients at room temperature. Heat oven to 350°F. Grease and flour a 13x9x2 inch baking pan, or two 8 or 9 inch layer pans. Sift together dry ingredients in large mixer bowl. Add remaining ingredients. Blend ½ minute on low speed, scraping bowl constantly. Beat 3 minutes on high speed, scraping bowl occasionally. Pour into pan(s). Bake in oblong pan 35 to 40 minutes, layer pans 30 to 35 minutes, or until wooden pick inserted in center comes out clean. Cool. Frost as desired. Serves 12.

FAVORITE COCOA CAKE

My friend Darlene's favorite cake!

1½ c. unsifted all-purpose flour	**1 Tbsp. distilled white vinegar**
1 c. firmly packed brown sugar	**1 c. milk**
⅓ c. unsweetened cocoa powder	**½ c. vegetable oil**
1 tsp. baking soda	**1 tsp. vanilla**
½ tsp. salt	

Grease 2 quart tube pan. Combine flour, brown sugar, cocoa, baking soda, salt, vinegar, and ½ cup of the milk in medium size bowl. Stir with spoon, about 100 strokes, until batter is smooth and stiff. Stir in remaining milk, oil, and vanilla until smooth and well blended. Pour batter into prepared pan. Bake in a 350° oven for 35 to 40 minutes or until cake tests done. Remove from oven. Let cake stand directly on heatproof board or counter until completely cool; the retained heat completes the cooking process. Sprinkle the top decoratively with (confectioners) sugar through a doily, or frost with your favorite icing, or serve plain with ice cream or whipped cream. Store the cake, covered, at room temperature. Serves 12.

DOUBLE CHOCOLATE CREAM CHEESE CAKE

Double good too!

Cake:

3 c. all-purpose flour
2 c. sugar
½ c. cocoa
2 tsp. soda
½ tsp. salt

2 c. hot coffee
⅔ c. oil
2 Tbsp. vinegar
2 tsp. vanilla
2 eggs

Filling:

⅓ c. sugar
8 oz. pkg. cream cheese, softened
½ tsp. vanilla
1 egg

6 oz. pkg. (1 c.) semi-sweet
  chocolate chips
1 c. finely chopped nuts
¼ c. sugar

Heat oven to 350°F. Grease and flour bottom only of 13x9 inch pan. Lightly spoon flour into measuring cup; level off. In large bowl, blend all cake ingredients at low speed until moistened; beat 1 minute at medium speed (batter will be thin). Pour into prepared pan. In small bowl, cream ⅓ cup sugar, cream cheese, ½ teaspoon vanilla, and 1 egg until fluffy; fold in chocolate chips and nuts. Spoon teaspoonfuls of filling evenly over batter; sprinkle with ¼ cup sugar. Bake at 350°F. for 45 to 60 minutes or until toothpick inserted in center comes out clean. Cool completely. Store in refrigerator. Makes 12 servings.

Tip: Self-rising flour is not recommended.

TUNNEL OF FUDGE CAKE

Since this cake has a soft tunnel of fudge, ordinary doneness test cannot be used - accurate oven temperature and bake time are critical.

Cake:

1¾ c. butter, softened
1¾ c. granulated sugar
6 eggs
2 c. confectioners sugar

2¼ c. all-purpose flour
¾ c. cocoa
2 c. chopped walnuts*

Glaze:

¾ c. confectioners sugar
¼ c. cocoa

1½ to 2 Tbsp. milk

Heat oven to 350°F. Grease and flour 12 cup fluted tube pan or 10 inch angel food tube pan. In large bowl, beat butter and granulated sugar until light and fluffy. Add eggs, one at a time, beating well after each addition. Gradually add confectioners sugar; blend well. By hand, stir in remaining cake ingredients until well blended. Spoon batter into prepared pan; spread evenly. Bake at 350°F. for 58 to 62 minutes. Cool upright in pan on cooling rack 1 hour; invert onto serving plate. Cool completely.

In small bowl, combine glaze ingredients until well blended. Spoon over top of cake, allowing some to run down sides. Store tightly covered. Makes 16 servings.

* Tip: Nuts are essential for the success of the recipe.

WELLESLEY FUDGE CAKE

This chocolate cake recipe is almost 100 years old.

4 sq. unsweetened chocolate	1 tsp. soda
½ c. hot water	½ c. butter
½ c. sugar	1¼ c. sugar
1 tsp. vanilla	3 eggs
1¾ c. sifted all-purpose flour*	¾ c. milk
1 tsp. baking soda	

Heat chocolate with water over very low heat, stirring until mixture is smooth. Add ½ cup sugar; cook and stir 2 minutes longer. Cool to lukewarm. Add vanilla.

Sift flour, soda, and salt. Cream butter. Gradually beat in the sugar; continue beating until fluffy. Beat eggs in thoroughly, one at a time. Add flour and milk alternately, beating after each addition until smooth. Blend in chocolate mixture. Pour into 2 greased and floured 9 inch layer pans. Bake at 350° for 30 to 35 minutes, or until cake tests done. Cool 10 minutes; remove from pans and finish cooling on racks. Fill and frost with Classic Fudge Frosting. Garnish if desired. Serves 12.

* Or use 2 cups sifted cake flour.

Classic Fudge Frosting: Melt 4 squares unsweetened chocolate and 2 tablespoons butter over very low heat. Combine 4 cups unsifted confectioners sugar, a dash of salt, ½ cup milk, and 1 teaspoon vanilla; add chocolate mixture, blending well.

Let stand, if necessary, until of spreading consistency, stirring occasionally. Spread quickly, adding a small amount of additional milk if frosting thickens. Makes about 2½ cups.

CHOCOLATE SHEET CAKE

Definitely an old timer.

1¼ c. butter	1 (14 oz.) can sweetened
½ c. unsweetened cocoa	condensed milk (not
1 c. water	evaporated milk)
2 c. unsifted flour	2 eggs
1½ c. firmly packed brown sugar	1 tsp. vanilla
1 tsp. baking soda	1 c. confectioners sugar
1 tsp. ground cinnamon	1 c. chopped nuts
½ tsp. salt	

Preheat oven to 350°. In small saucepan, melt 1 cup butter; stir in ¼ cup cocoa then water. Bring to a boil; remove from heat. In large mixer bowl, combine flour, brown sugar, baking soda, cinnamon, and salt. Add cocoa mixture; beat well. Stir in ⅓ cup condensed milk, eggs, and vanilla. Pour into greased 15x10 inch jelly roll pan. Bake for 15 minutes or until cake springs back when lightly touched. In small saucepan, melt remaining ¼ cup butter; stir in remaining ¼ cup cocoa and condensed milk. Stir in confectioners sugar and nuts. Spread on warm cake. Serves 12.

PETITE SPICE CAKES

These are delicious little cakes, drizzled with chocolate.

2 eggs	1½ c. granulated sugar
1 c. granulated sugar	¾ c. hot water
1 c. all-purpose flour	1 tsp. finely shredded lemon peel
1 tsp. baking powder	¼ tsp. cream of tartar
½ tsp. ground cardamom	1 tsp. vanilla
¼ tsp. salt	Sifted confectioners sugar (about
½ c. milk	1¼ c.)
2 Tbsp. butter	Melted German's sweet chocolate

Grease and lightly flour a 9x9x2 inch baking pan; set aside. In a small mixer bowl, beat the eggs with an electric mixer on high speed for about 4 minutes or till the eggs are thick and lemon colored. Gradually add the 1 cup granulated sugar, beating on medium speed for 4 to 5 minutes or till the sugar is nearly dissolved. In a mixing bowl, stir together the flour, baking powder, cardamom, and salt. Add the dry ingredients to the beaten egg mixture; stir just till the mixture is blended.

In a small saucepan, heat the milk and butter till the butter melts; stir into the batter in mixer bowl. Beat mixture on low speed till well mixed. Turn the cake batter into the prepared baking pan. Bake in a 350° oven for 25 to 30 minutes or till the cake tests done. Cool cake in pan for 10 minutes on a wire rack. Remove cake from pan; cool thoroughly on wire rack before icing.

For vanilla icing: In a 1 quart saucepan, stir together the 1½ cups granulated sugar, the hot water, and shredded lemon peel, and cream of tartar. Cover and bring the mixture to boiling. Uncover; clip a candy thermometer to the saucepan. Cook over medium low heat till the temperature registers 226°. Remove the saucepan from heat. Cool mixture, without stirring, to 110° (about 45 minutes). Stir in the vanilla. Stir in enough sifted confectioners sugar to make a pourable consistency. Beat the icing in saucepan till smooth.

Using a knife or cookie cutter, cut the cake into shapes such as squares, diamonds, and circles that are about 1½ inches wide. Place the cake pieces on a wire rack over waxed paper. Spoon the vanilla icing over the small cakes to coat evenly. Drizzle melted chocolate atop each iced cake to form a design. Chill the decorated cakes a few minutes to firm the drizzled chocolate. Makes about 16 small cakes.

Note: For best cooking results, check the accuracy of your candy thermometer before each use. To test, place the candy thermometer in a saucepan of boiling water. If the thermometer registers either above or below 212°, add or subtract the same number of degrees from the recipe temperature and cook to that temperature. For added accuracy, read the candy thermometer at eye level while clipped to the saucepan on the range top.

When clipping the candy thermometer to side of the saucepan, make sure the bulb of the thermometer is completely covered with the boiling liquid, not just foam, and that the bulb doesn't touch the bottom of the saucepan. This ensures a more exact reading.

MINI-CHIP POUND CAKE

This cake freezes very well.

2 c. all-purpose flour
½ tsp. baking powder
½ tsp. salt
1 c. (6 oz.) semi-sweet chocolate
   mini chips

1 c. butter (at room temperature)
1 c. granulated sugar
5 large eggs
2 tsp. ground ginger or vanilla
Confectioners sugar (optional)

Heat oven to 325°. Grease and lightly flour a 9 inch fluted or plain tube pan. Mix flour, baking powder, salt, and chocolate chips. In a large bowl, beat butter with electric mixer until smooth. Gradually beat in sugar until mixture is pale and fluffy. Add eggs one at a time, beating well after each. Beat in ginger. Stir in flour mixture until well blended. Turn into prepared tube pan. Bake 65 minutes or until pick inserted in center of cake comes out clean and cake pulls away from sides of pan. Cool in pan on rack 10 minutes, then unmold onto rack. Sprinkle with confectioners sugar if desired. Serves 12.

MOCHA CHIP CUPCAKES

Children adore these heavenly cupcakes. Grownups do too!

Dissolve 1 tablespoon instant coffee crystals in ½ cup milk. Cream together ½ cup sugar, 6 tablespoons butter, 1 egg, and 1 egg yolk, beating till fluffy. Blend in 1 (1 ounce) square unsweetened chocolate, melted and cooled. Stir together 1 cup all-purpose flour, 1 teaspoon baking powder, ¼ teaspoon salt, and ¼ teaspoon baking soda; add to creamed mixture alternately with milk mixture. Fill 12 muffin pans lined with paper bake cups ⅔ full with batter. Bake in 375° oven for 12 minutes. Meanwhile, in small mixer bowl, beat together 1 egg white and 1 teaspoon instant coffee crystals, crushed, to soft peaks. Gradually add ⅓ cup sugar, beating till stiff peaks form. Fold in ½ of 6 ounce package (½ cup) semi-sweet chocolate pieces and ½ cup chopped walnuts. Carefully spoon 1 tablespoon meringue atop each partially baked cupcake. Bake 10 to 12 minutes longer or till lightly browned. Makes 12.

15

NO-BAKE BLACK FOREST REFRIGERATOR CAKE

Prepare this easy-to-put-together cake, with store-bought ladyfingers and a no-bake chocolate filling, a day ahead. Unmold just before serving.

10 ladyfingers, split in halves
⅓ c. evaporated milk
½ tsp. lemon juice
2 egg whites
⅛ tsp. salt
2 Tbsp. cold water
2 Tbsp. cherry flavored liqueur or water

1 env. unflavored gelatin
⅔ c. strong coffee
4 ice cubes
3 (.75 oz.) pkg. chocolate dairy drink mix
2 tsp. vanilla
1 c. fresh or frozen cherries, thawed

1. Line bottom and long sides of 8½ x 4½ x 2 inch glass loaf pan with one long sheet of wax paper, extending the ends of the paper several inches beyond the rims. Arrange 6 ladyfinger halves, flat side up, across the bottom, parallel to the short ends of the dish. Line each long side of the pan with 7 ladyfinger halves, standing up with flat sides facing in. Set aside.

2. Place medium size bowl in freezer along with mixer beaters. Pour evaporated milk into ice cube trays. Place in freezer until ice crystals form around the edges, about 25 minutes.

3. Scoop out the evaporated milk into the chilled bowl. Add lemon juice. Beat with chilled beaters until stiff. Reserve.

4. Beat egg whites and salt in second bowl until stiff peaks form. Reserve.

5. Combine cold water and cherry flavored liqueur in container of electric blender. Sprinkle gelatin over liquid; allow to soften about 1 minute.

6. Meanwhile, heat coffee to boiling in small saucepan. Pour over softened gelatin. Cover container; whirl until gelatin is dissolved. Add ice cubes, chocolate dairy drink mix, and vanilla. Cover; whirl until well mixed. Transfer to large bowl. If mixture has not begun to set, chill just until it does.

7. Fold whipped evaporated milk and beaten egg whites into chocolate mixture. Spoon chocolate filling into the ladyfinger lined baking dish.

8. With a serrated knife, carefully trim ends of ladyfingers even with top of filling. Sprinkle trimmed pieces evenly over top of filling. Bring ends of wax paper over top; cover entire top lightly with plastic wrap. Refrigerate overnight.

9. To unmold, carefully invert dish onto serving plate. Remove dish and wax paper. Garnish top of cake with whole cherries. Serve immediately. Serves 10.

BROWNIE SHEET CAKE

Freeze frosted cake up to 1 month. Decorate night before; return to refrigerator.

Cake:

2 c. butter	2 c. all-purpose flour
2 (12 oz.) pkg. semi-sweet chocolate mini chips (4 c.)	2 c. hazelnuts or walnuts, chopped coarse
2⅔ c. granulated sugar	Chocolate Frosting (recipe follows)
4 tsp. vanilla	For decorating: White ready-to-pipe icing
8 large eggs	

Heat oven to 350°. Lightly grease a 14x10x2 inch roasting pan. Line with 2 sheets waxed paper; grease paper and dust lightly with flour. Melt butter in Dutch oven or 6 quart saucepot over medium low heat. Add chocolate chips and stir until melted. Remove from heat. Stir in sugar and vanilla with wooden spoon until blended. Add eggs one at a time, stirring briskly until each is incorporated before adding the next. Gradually stir in flour until blended. Stir in nuts. Spread batter evenly in lined pan and bake for 60 to 65 minutes until a toothpick inserted in the center comes out almost clean (cake should be moist in middle). Cool in pan on rack to room temperature, about 1½ hours. Line cookie sheet with waxed paper. Invert cake onto lined sheet; lift off pan and peel off waxed paper. Prepare Chocolate Frosting; pour warm frosting over cake and spread evenly over top and sides with long metal spatula. Freeze cake until frosting is hard to the touch, then wrap airtight, leaving cake on the waxed paper. Return cake to freezer. To serve, the night before, remove cake from freezer. Unwrap and run sharp knife between waxed paper and cake. Lift cake to serving tray, platter, or board. Decorate cake and refrigerate. Remove from refrigerator 1 hour before guests arrive. Cut into 24 pieces.

Chocolate Frosting: Pour 1 (12 ounce) package semi-sweet chocolate mini chips (2 cups) into a large bowl. Have a hand held or stand model electric mixer handy. Bring ¾ cup heavy cream to a full boil in a small saucepan. Gradually pour hot cream over chocolate, starting to beat with mixer on low speed as soon as cream touches chocolate. Continue beating until chocolate is completely melted and mixture is smooth, 1 to 2 minutes. Makes 1¾ cakes.

BABY BROWNIE CAKES

Mini cakes: Little - but luscious!

¾ c. butter	2 tsp. vanilla
4 (1 oz.) sq. unsweetened chocolate	1 c. all-purpose flour
3 eggs	1 c. chopped walnuts or pecans
¼ tsp. salt	Chocolate Glaze (recipe follows)
1½ c. sugar	White chocolate, melted (optional)

1. Preheat oven to moderate (350°). Line eighteen 2½ inch muffin pan cups with paper or foil baking cups.

2. Melt together butter and chocolate in top of double boiler over hot water. Let cool slightly.

3. Beat together eggs and salt in large bowl until foamy. Gradually add sugar and beat until thick and pale yellow, about 3 to 5 minutes. Beat in vanilla. Blend in melted chocolate mixture. Add flour, stirring just until combined. Stir in nuts. Spoon into lined cups, dividing batter equally.

4. Bake in preheated moderate oven (350°) for 20 to 25 minutes or until wooden pick inserted in centers comes out slightly moist. Remove cakes to wire rack to cool.

5. Frost tops with Chocolate Glaze. Drizzle with melted white chocolate, if you wish. Makes 18 cups.

Chocolate Glaze for Baby Brownie Cakes: Melt together 1 (4 ounce) package sweet cooking chocolate, coarsely chopped, and ⅓ cup heavy cream in top of double boiler over hot water, stirring until smooth. Remove from heat. Makes about ¾ cup.

CHOCOLATE-CREAM CHEESE CUPCAKES

Makes enough for 18 chocolate hungry people!

Cream Cheese Filling (recipe
   follows)
1½ c. unsifted all-purpose flour
1 c. sugar
¼ c. unsweetened cocoa powder
1 tsp. baking soda

½ tsp. salt
1 c. water
⅓ c. vegetable oil
1 Tbsp. distilled white vinegar
1 tsp. vanilla

1. Preheat oven to moderate (350°). Line eighteen 2½ inch muffin pan cups with foil or paper baking cups.

2. Prepare Cream Cheese Filling. Set aside.

3. Sift together flour, sugar, cocoa powder, baking soda, and salt into large bowl.

4. Combine water, oil, vinegar, and vanilla in small bowl. Stir into flour mixture until blended.

5. Half fill each lined muffin pan cup with batter. Place spoonful of Cream Cheese Filling into center of batter in each cup.

6. Bake in preheated moderate oven (350°) for 25 to 30 minutes or until wooden pick inserted into chocolate part comes out clean. Remove pans from oven and let cakes cool in pans 5 to 10 minutes. Remove from pans to wire racks to cool completely. Makes 18 mini cakes.

Cream Cheese Filling: Beat 1 (8 ounce) package cream cheese (softened), 1 egg, and ¼ cup sugar in bowl until smooth. Stir in 1 cup (6 ounce package) semi-sweet chocolate pieces. Makes about 2 cups.

PIES AND THEIR CRUSTS

CHOCOLATE WHIPPED CREAM PIE

An intensely chocolate version of an all-American favorite.

2 c. milk
½ c. sugar
3 Tbsp. cornstarch
2 eggs
10 (1 oz.) sq. semi-sweet chocolate,
   coarsely chopped

¼ c. (½ stick) butter, cut into Tbsp.
2 c. heavy cream
1 baked 9 inch pie crust shell

Heat milk to boiling in large heavy saucepan. Stir together sugar and cornstarch in a medium size bowl; beat in eggs until smooth. Slowly stir in half the boiling milk; return to saucepan. Heat to boiling, stirring constantly; boil 1 minute. Remove from heat.

Stir chocolate pieces and butter into custard until melted. Gradually stir in 1 cup of the cream. Pour chocolate filling into baked pie shell. Lay a sheet of wax paper loosely over filling; cool. Refrigerate overnight. Remove wax paper from pie. Whip remaining 1 cup cream in small bowl until stiff; spread over pie, forming swirls with a knife or spatula. Serves 8.

CHOCOLATE WALNUT PIE

A recipe worth keeping a secret.

2 eggs
½ c. all-purpose flour
½ c. sugar
½ c. brown sugar, firmly packed
1 c. butter, melted and cooled to
   room temperature

1 (6 oz.) pkg. (1 c.) semi-sweet
   chocolate bits
1 c. chopped walnuts
1 (9 inch) unbaked pie shell
Whipped cream or ice cream
   (optional)

Preheat oven to 325°F. In large bowl, beat eggs until foamy; add flour, sugar, and brown sugar. Beat until well blended. Blend in melted butter. Stir in semi-sweet chocolate bits and walnuts. Pour into pie shell. Bake at 325°F. for 1 hour. Remove from oven. Serve warm with whipped cream or ice cream. Makes one 9 inch pie.

Recipe may be doubled. Bake two pies; freeze one for later use.

RUM CREAM PIE

With a chocolate crust and a rum flavored filling, Rum Cream Pie is irresistible.

1½ c. chocolate wafer crumbs
¼ c. plus 2 Tbsp. butter, melted
1½ tsp. unflavored gelatin
¼ c. water
3 egg yolks
½ c. sugar

¼ c. light rum
1 c. whipping cream, whipped
Coarsely grated chocolate
   (optional)
Chocolate curls (optional)

Combine chocolate crumbs and butter, mixing well. Place crumb mixture in a 9 inch pie plate and press onto bottom and sides to form an even crust. Chill 1 hour.

Combine gelatin and water in a small saucepan; let stand 1 minute. Cook over medium heat, stirring constantly, until gelatin dissolves; set aside to cool.

Beat egg yolks and sugar until thick and lemon colored. Gradually stir gelatin mixture into yolk mixture; beat well. Stir in rum; fold in whipped cream. Pour mixture into chilled pastry. Chill pie until firm. Top with grated chocolate and chocolate curls if desired. Serves 8 to 10.

COLONIAL INNKEEPER'S PIE

A traditional chocolate pie.

1½ oz. unsweetened chocolate	1 tsp. baking powder
½ c. water	½ tsp. salt
⅔ c. sugar	½ c. milk
8 Tbsp. (1 stick) butter (room temperature)	1 egg
	1 unbaked 9 inch pie shell
2 tsp. vanilla	½ c. chopped walnuts
1 c. all-purpose flour	1 c. whipping cream, whipped
¾ c. sugar	

Preheat oven to 350°F. Melt chocolate with water in small saucepan over hot water, stirring frequently. Add ⅔ cup sugar. Remove from over water; increase heat to medium high and bring to boil, stirring constantly. Remove from heat. Add 4 tablespoons butter and stir until melted. Add 1½ teaspoons vanilla. Set aside.

Combine flour, ¾ cup sugar, baking powder, and salt in medium bowl of electric mixer. Add milk and remaining butter and vanilla and beat 2 minutes. Add egg and beat 2 more minutes. Pour batter into pie shell. Stir chocolate sauce and carefully pour over batter. Sprinkle with nuts. Bake until tester inserted in center comes out clean, about 55 minutes. Serve warm or at room temperature with whipped cream. Serves 8.

GERMAN CHOCOLATE PIE

Guaranteed to cure your chocolate hunger!

⅓ c. sugar	1 beaten egg
3 Tbsp. cornstarch	1 (5⅓ oz.) can evaporated milk (⅔ c.)
1½ c. milk	
1 (4 oz.) bar German's sweet cooking chocolate, cut up	½ c. sugar
	¼ c. butter
1 Tbsp. butter	1 (3½ oz.) can flaked coconut (1⅓ c.)
2 beaten egg yolks	
1 tsp. vanilla	½ c. chopped pecans
1 (9 inch) baked pie shell	

In a medium saucepan, combine the ⅓ cup sugar and the cornstarch. Stir in the milk, chocolate, and 1 tablespoon butter. Cook and stir till thickened and bubbly.

20

Reduce heat; cook and stir 2 minutes more. Gradually stir about 1 cup of the hot mixture into egg yolks. Return mixture to saucepan; bring to boiling. Cook and stir 2 minutes more. Stir in vanilla. Turn the hot pie filling into the baked pie shell.

In another saucepan, combine the beaten egg, evaporated milk, the ½ cup sugar, and ¼ cup butter. Cook and stir over medium heat just till the mixture is thickened and bubbly. Stir in the coconut and pecans. Spread the pecan mixture evenly over the chocolate filling. Cool the pie on a wire rack; chill thoroughly. Makes 10 servings.

CHOCOLATE CHEESE PIE

Let the children lick the chocolate pie bowls.

6 oz. semi-sweet chocolate pieces	1 tsp. vanilla
6 oz. pkg. cream cheese, softened	2 eggs, separated
¾ c. light brown sugar	1 c. heavy cream, whipped
⅛ tsp. salt	9 inch graham cracker pie crust

Melt chocolate over hot water, not boiling. Cool about 10 minutes. Blend cream cheese, ½ cup sugar, salt, and vanilla. Beat in egg yolks, one at a time. Beat in cooled chocolate; blend well. Beat egg whites until stiff but not dry. Gradually add remaining ¼ cup sugar and beat until egg whites are stiff and glossy. Fold chocolate mixture into beaten egg whites. Fold in whipped cream. Pour into chilled crust; reserve ¼ of mixture for decorating. Chill until filling sets slightly. With tapered spoon, drop remaining mixture in mounds over top. Chill overnight. Serves 8.

CHOCOLATE COCONUT PIE

A crustless chocolate pie. Put it in a crust if you like.

3 sq. unsweetened chocolate	½ c. all-purpose flour
½ c. butter	1 tsp. vanilla
3 eggs, slightly beaten	⅔ c. sweetened condensed milk
¾ c. sugar	2⅔ c. flaked coconut

Melt chocolate and butter in saucepan over low heat. Stir in eggs, sugar, flour, and vanilla. Pour into greased 9 inch pie pan. Combine milk and coconut; spoon over chocolate mixture, leaving a ½ to 1 inch border. Bake at 350° for 30 minutes. Serves 8.

CHOCOLATE SWIRL CHEESE PIE

A very rich chocolate pie.

1 c. sugar	1 Tbsp. vanilla
3 (8 oz.) pkg. cream cheese, softened	1 (4 oz.) pkg. sweet chocolate, melted and cooled
5 eggs	

Add sugar to cheese in a bowl, beating well. Add eggs, one at a time, beating well after each addition. Add vanilla. Measure 2 cups of the cheese mixture; fold in chocolate. Pour remaining cheese mixture into well buttered 10 inch pie pan or 9 inch square pan. Add spoonfuls of the chocolate-cheese mixture and zigzag a spatula through batter to marble. Bake at 350° for 40 to 45 minutes. Cool, then chill. Cut in wedges. Serves 10.

COOKIES, BARS, AND SQUARES

CHOCO-PEANUT BUTTER POPS

Chocolate lollipops for children and grownup chocolate lovers!

In small bowl, combine ½ cup chunky peanut butter and ¼ cup grape jelly. Spread ½ chocolate wafer cookies with peanut butter and jelly mixture; top each with additional chocolate wafer to make 12 cookie sandwiches. Insert popsicle stick into filling of each cookie sandwich to make lollipop; set aside. In small heavy saucepan over very low heat, melt four 1 ounce squares semi-sweet or 4 ounces milk chocolate and 1 teaspoon butter, stirring frequently, until blended and smooth. Dip lollipops into chocolate mixture to coat completely; place on wax paper lined cookie sheet. Refrigerate at least 20 minutes until chocolate coating is set. Makes 12 lollipops.

CHOCOLATE BIRTHDAY TEDDY BEARS

For a delightful children's birthday party, serve ice cream cups, complete with candles, with these teddy bear cookies decorated with each child's name.

1 c. sugar
½ c. butter (1 stick), softened
2 c. all-purpose flour
2 tsp. vanilla
½ tsp. baking soda
½ tsp. salt
2 sq. unsweetened chocolate, melted
2 eggs
Decorator's Frosting

About 4 hours before serving or early in day:

1. In large bowl, with mixer at high speed, beat sugar and butter until light and fluffy. Reduce speed to low; add flour, vanilla, baking soda, salt, melted chocolate, and eggs; beat ingredients until well mixed, occasionally scraping bowl with rubber spatula.

2. Shape dough into ball; wrap with plastic wrap and refrigerate 2 hours or until dough is easy to handle. (Or, place dough in freezer 40 minutes.)

3. Preheat oven to 350°F. Divide dough into 12 pieces. Cut one dough piece in half. Shape half into a large ball for bear's body; place on ungreased cookie sheet. Flatten slightly into 3 x 2½ inch oval. Cut remaining half in half; shape one piece into small ball. Arrange next to large ball, slightly overlapping it for bear's head. From remaining dough, pinch off a small piece for nose; place on head. Roll remaining piece into 5 inch long rope. Cut two ½ inch pieces for ears and cut four 1 inch pieces for legs; roll each into a ball. Place ears and legs next to bear. Repeat with remaining dough to make 12 bears in all. Bake 8 minutes or until cookies are almost set. Cool cookies on cookie sheet on wire rack.

4. When cookies are cool, prepare Decorator's Frosting. Use frosting in decorating bag to decorate cookies as desired. Makes 1 dozen.

Decorators Frosting: In small bowl, with mixer at low speed, beat 1¼ cups confectioners sugar, ⅛ teaspoon cream of tartar, and 1 egg white until blended. Increase speed to high; beat mixture until so stiff that knife drawn through mixture leaves a clean-cut path. Makes about 1½ cups.

MINI CHOCOLATE BOURBON BITES

The addition of bourbon to these cookies makes them extra special.

½ c. butter
½ c. packed brown sugar
¼ c. bourbon
1 c. all-purpose flour
3 Tbsp. unsweetened cocoa powder

½ c. miniature semi-sweet
chocolate pieces
1 slightly beaten egg white
1 c. finely chopped pecans

In a large mixer bowl, beat butter and sugar with electric mixer on medium speed till fluffy. Add bourbon; beat well. Gradually add flour and cocoa powder, beating till well mixed. Stir in chocolate pieces. Chill 2 hours or till firm enough to handle.

Shape dough into 1 inch balls. Roll in egg white, then in nuts. Place on a lightly greased baking sheet. Bake in a 350° oven for about 12 minutes or till edges are firm. (The center will still be soft.) Cool on baking sheet 1 minute. Cool on wire racks. Makes about 30.

BLACK AND WHITE ALMOND MACAROONS

By adding a bit of chocolate to almond macaroons, we've provided a striking contrast in flavor and color.

2 (4 oz.) cans blanched slivered
almonds
Confectioners sugar
2 egg whites (at room temperature)
⅛ tsp. cream of tartar

2 tsp. almond extract
½ tsp. vanilla
½ c. flaked coconut
1 sq. unsweetened chocolate,
melted

About 1½ hours before serving or early in day:

1. In blender at medium speed, blend almonds and ¼ cup confectioners sugar, in batches, until finely ground; place in large bowl. (Or, blend almonds and confectioners sugar in food processor.)

2. In small bowl, with mixer at high speed, beat egg whites and cream of tartar until soft peaks form. Beating at high speed, sprinkle in ½ cup confectioners sugar, 2 tablespoons at a time, beating well after each addition until sugar is completely dissolved; beat in almond and vanilla extracts. (Whites should stand in stiff, glossy peaks.) With rubber spatula, fold egg whites and coconut into ground almonds. Measure ⅔ cup of cookie mixture into small bowl. With rubber spatula, fold in melted chocolate.

3. Preheat oven to 325°F. Grease large cookie sheets. Fill tablespoon, two-thirds full, with white cookie mixture. With small metal spatula, place a dab of chocolate mixture in remaining one-third of spoon; round mixtures without smearing them together. With spatula pushing mixture from chocolate side, drop cookies, about 1 inch apart, onto prepared cookie sheets. Bake about 20 minutes or until cookies are lightly browned on bottoms. With pancake turner, remove cookies to wire racks to cool. Store cookies in tightly covered container. Makes about 2 dozen cookies.

WALNUT-CREAM CHEESE BROWNIES

A rich chocolate brownie.

4 (1 oz.) sq. unsweetened chocolate
¾ c. butter, softened
2 c. sugar
3 eggs
1 c. all-purpose flour
½ tsp. salt
1 c. chopped walnuts or pecans

1 tsp. vanilla
1 (8 oz.) pkg. cream cheese,
   softened
½ c. sugar
1 egg
1 tsp. vanilla

Melt chocolate in top of a double boiler over hot water; set aside to cool. Cream butter; gradually add 2 cups sugar, beating well. Add 3 eggs, one at a time, beating well after each addition. Stir melted chocolate into butter mixture. Add flour, salt, walnuts, and 1 teaspoon vanilla, stirring well. Pour batter into a greased and floured 13x9x2 inch baking pan; set aside.

Beat cream cheese until smooth; gradually add ½ cup sugar, beating well. Add 1 egg and 1 teaspoon vanilla, beating well. Drop mixture by heaping tablespoonfuls over chocolate mixture. Swirl cream cheese mixture into chocolate mixture with a knife. Bake at 350° for 45 minutes. Cool and cut into squares. Makes 3½ dozen.

MERINGUE-TOPPED BROWNIES

Brownies made a different way.

½ c. butter
2 sq. (2 oz.) unsweetened chocolate
¾ c. granulated sugar
1 egg
1 egg yolk
1 tsp. vanilla

1 c. all-purpose flour
½ tsp. baking powder
1 egg white
½ c. packed brown sugar
¼ c. chopped walnuts

Melt butter and chocolate. Remove from heat; stir in sugar. Add egg, yolk, and vanilla; mix. Combine flour and baking powder; stir into chocolate mixture. Spread in greased 8x8x2 inch baking pan. Beat egg white till soft peaks form. Gradually add brown sugar. Beat till very stiff peaks form. Spread meringue over batter. Sprinkle with nuts. Bake at 350° for 30 to 35 minutes. Cool. Makes 16 bars.

COCOA KISS COOKIES

A favorite chocolate cookie.

1 c. butter, softened
⅔ c. sugar
1 tsp. vanilla
1⅔ c. all-purpose flour

¼ c. cocoa
1 c. coarsely ground walnuts
1 (9 oz.) pkg. milk chocolate
   Kisses, unwrapped

Cream butter; gradually add sugar, beating until light and fluffy. Add vanilla, mixing well. Add flour and cocoa, mixing well. Stir in walnuts. Chill dough 2 hours or until firm.

Wrap 1 tablespoon of dough around each chocolate Kiss, and roll to form a ball. Place on ungreased cookie sheets and bake at 375° for 12 minutes. Cool slightly on cookie sheets; remove to wire racks. Makes about 4 dozen.

THE DEEP-DISH BROWNIE

Makes just one serving for true chocoholics!

¾ c. butter, melted
1½ c. sugar
1½ tsp. vanilla
3 eggs

¾ c. unsifted all-purpose flour
½ c. cocoa
½ tsp. baking powder
½ tsp. salt

Blend melted butter, sugar, and vanilla in a mixing bowl. Add eggs; beat well with spoon. Combine flour, cocoa, baking powder, and salt. Gradually add to egg mixture until well blended. Spread in greased 8 inch square pan. Bake at 350°F. for 40 to 45 minutes or until brownie begins to pull away from edges of pan. Cool; cut into squares. Makes 16 squares.

FUDGY FRUITCAKE DROPS

Raisins, walnuts, and jelly are among the ingredients used in these special cookies.

¼ c. butter
½ c. sugar
1 egg
½ c. grape jelly
1 tsp. vanilla
1 c. all-purpose flour
¼ c. unsweetened cocoa powder

2 tsp. baking powder
2 c. chopped walnuts (8 oz.)
1½ c. raisins (8 oz.)
1 (6 oz.) pkg. (1 c.) semi-sweet
   chocolate pieces
Confectioners sugar (optional)

In a large mixer bowl, beat butter for 30 seconds; add sugar. Beat till fluffy. Add egg, grape jelly, and vanilla; beat till well blended. Stir together flour, cocoa powder, and baking powder. Stir flour mixture into beaten mixture. Stir in nuts, raisins, and chocolate pieces. Drop by rounded teaspoonfuls onto greased and floured baking sheets. Bake in 350° oven for about 10 minutes or till just set. Cool 1 minute. Remove to wire rack to cool. If desired, sift confectioners sugar over cooled cookies. Makes about 50 cookies.

ALMOND CHIP BALLS

A just delicious chocolate cookie.

1 c. all-purpose flour
½ c. miniature semi-sweet
   chocolate morsels
½ c. chopped almonds, toasted
½ c. butter, softened

2 Tbsp. sugar
1 Tbsp. brown sugar
1 tsp. vanilla extract
Sifted confectioners sugar
   (optional)

Combine first 7 ingredients; mix well. Shape into ¾ inch balls. Place on ungreased cookie sheets; bake at 350° for 12 to 15 minutes. Remove cookies to wire racks to cool. Coat warm cookies with confectioners sugar if desired. Makes about 2½ dozen.

SAUCEPAN PRETZEL BROWNIES

Yes, pretzels in brownies!

⅔ c. shortening
4 (1 oz.) sq. unsweetened chocolate
4 eggs, beaten
2 c. sugar

1 c. all-purpose flour
1 tsp. baking powder
1 c. finely crushed pretzels
1 c. coarsely chopped walnuts

Melt shortening and chocolate in a large saucepan over low heat. Combine eggs and sugar, mixing until blended. Add to chocolate mixture, beating until smooth. Add remaining ingredients, mixing well (batter will be very stiff).

Spread mixture in a well greased 13x9x2 inch baking pan. Bake at 350° for 30 minutes or until center is firm. Cool in pan on wire rack. Cut into squares. Makes 32 squares.

DOUBLE CHOCOLATE CHIP COOKIES

Crisp on the outside, chewy in the middle.

2 c. all-purpose flour
¼ c. unsweetened cocoa powder
½ tsp. salt
1 c. butter (at room temperature)
¾ c. granulated sugar
¾ c. packed brown sugar
2 large eggs

1 tsp. vanilla
1 tsp. baking soda
1 Tbsp. hot water
2 c. chopped walnuts
2 c. (12 oz.) semi-sweet chocolate
  chips

Heat oven to 375°. Lightly grease 2 cookie sheets. Mix flour, cocoa, and salt. In a large bowl, beat butter with electric mixer until smooth. Add sugars; beat until blended. Add eggs and vanilla; beat until pale and fluffy. In a bowl, mix baking soda and water. Stir half the flour mixture into sugar mixture; beat in dissolved baking soda, then stir in remaining flour mixture until well blended. Stir in walnuts and chocolate chips. Drop heaping teaspoonfuls of dough 2 inches apart on prepared cookie sheets. Bake one sheet at a time for 10 to 12 minutes until cookies look firm. Cool on sheet 1 minute before removing to racks to cool completely. Makes 80.

DOUBLE CHIP COOKIES

Fill the cookie jar with these delicious cookies.

¾ c. butter, softened
¼ c. shortening
1 c. sugar
½ c. firmly packed brown sugar
2 eggs
1 tsp. vanilla

2¼ c. all-purpose flour
1 tsp. baking soda
½ tsp. salt
1 (6 oz.) pkg. peanut butter morsels
1 (6 oz.) pkg. semi-sweet chocolate
  morsels

Cream butter and shortening; gradually add sugars, beating until light and fluffy. Add eggs and vanilla, beating well.

Combine flour, soda, and salt; add to creamed mixture, beating well. Stir in peanut butter and chocolate morsels.

Drop dough by heaping teaspoonfuls onto ungreased cookie sheets. Bake at 350° for 12 to 14 minutes. Cool slightly on cookie sheets; remove to wire racks to cool completely. Makes about 5½ dozen.

CHOCOLATE MELTAWAYS

They will melt in your mouth!

¾ c. butter, softened
1 c. sugar
1 egg
2 (1 oz.) env. liquid baking
   chocolate
2 Tbsp. milk

1 tsp. vanilla
2 c. all-purpose flour
¼ tsp. salt
½ c. chocolate drink mix
½ c. chopped pecans or walnuts

Cream butter; gradually add sugar, beating until light and fluffy. Add next 4 ingredients and beat well.

Combine flour and salt; gradually add to creamed mixture, beating just until smooth. Chill dough 1 to 2 hours.

Combine drink mix and pecans. Shape dough into ¾ inch balls; roll in pecan mixture. Place on ungreased cookie sheets. Bake at 350° for 10 minutes. Cool on wire racks. Makes about 5 dozen cookies.

CHOCOLATE CHERRY SQUARES

A nice holiday sweet treat. For children's gifts or hostess gifts, put in a plastic bag and tie with a pretty ribbon with the recipe.

1 c. unsifted all-purpose flour
½ c. packed light brown sugar
⅓ c. cold butter
½ c. chopped nuts
1 (8 oz.) pkg. cream cheese,
   softened
½ c. sugar

⅓ c. cocoa
¼ c. milk
1 egg
½ tsp. vanilla
½ c. chopped red candied cherries
Red candied cherries, halved

Combine flour, brown sugar, and butter (cut into chunks) in large mixer bowl. Blend on low speed to form fine crumbs, about 2 to 3 minutes. Stir in nuts. Reserve ¾ cup crumb mixture for topping; press remaining crumbs into ungreased 9 inch square pan. Bake at 350° for 10 minutes or until lightly browned. Meanwhile, combine cream cheese, sugar, cocoa, milk, egg, and vanilla in small mixer bowl; beat until smooth. Fold in cherries. Spread mixture over warm crust. Sprinkle reserved crumb mixture over top; garnish with cherry halves. Return to oven; continue to bake at 350° for 25 minutes or until lightly browned and filling is set. Cool; cut into squares. Store in refrigerator. Makes about 3 dozen squares.

AUNT BETTY'S BROWNIES

The pecan halves rise during baking to make a crunchy topping. A "Texas brownie" made with those fine paper shell pecans.

Butter	2 tsp. vanilla
Flour	2 eggs, beaten to blend
½ c. (1 stick) butter	½ c. all-purpose flour
1 c. sugar	1½ c. pecan halves
3 Tbsp. unsweetened cocoa powder	Confectioners sugar (optional)

Preheat oven to 350°F. Butter and flour 7 x 10 x ¾ inch metal pan. Melt ½ cup butter with sugar, cocoa powder, and vanilla in heavy medium saucepan over low heat, stirring occasionally. Cool. Mix in eggs and flour until just blended. Stir in pecans. Pour into prepared pan. Bake until brownies start to pull away from sides of pan, about 25 minutes. Cool in pan 30 minutes. Turn out onto rack and cool completely. Cut into 2 inch squares. (Can be prepared 2 days ahead. Wrap tightly.) Just before serving, dust with confectioners sugar if desired. Makes about 15 squares.

HEAVENLY OATMEAL BARS

Crisp, buttery oatmeal bars with a thick, creamy chocolate and peanut butter glaze; they're a specialty.

1 c. unsalted butter	3⅓ c. quick cooking oats
1⅓ c. packed dark brown sugar	2 tsp. vanilla
¼ c. light corn syrup	Glaze (recipe follows)

Heat oven to 350°. Grease a 13x9 inch baking pan. Beat butter and sugar in a large bowl with electric mixer until fluffy. Stir in corn syrup, oats, and vanilla with wooden spoon. With buttered fingers pat mixture evenly into prepared pan. Bake in middle of oven for 16 minutes. (Dough will still look moist near center. Don't overbake.) Cool in pan on rack until lukewarm, then spread warm glaze over top. Cool completely (may be refrigerated) before cutting into 2x1 inch bars. Makes 48.

Glaze: Put 2 cups (12 ounces) semi-sweet chocolate chips and 1 cup creamy peanut butter in a small saucepan. Stir over low heat until chocolate melts and mixture is smooth. Makes 3 cups.

CHOCOLATE CHOCOLATE CHIP COOKIES

The dough for these cookies can be prepared one day ahead.

1 c. (2 sticks) unsalted butter (room temperature)	3 c. sifted all-purpose flour
	1 tsp. baking powder
⅔ c. firmly packed brown sugar	1 tsp. cinnamon
⅔ c. sugar	¼ tsp. freshly grated nutmeg
1 extra large egg, beaten to blend	6 oz. semi-sweet chocolate chips
6 oz. semi-sweet chocolate chips, melted and cooled	

Cream butter with sugars in large bowl of electric mixer until light and fluffy. Beat in egg and melted chocolate. Sift flour with baking powder, cinnamon, and nutmeg. Add to butter mixture on low speed until just blended. Stir in remaining 6 ounces chocolate chips. Cover and refrigerate 1 hour.

To form and bake cookies: Shape chilled dough into smooth 16 inch cylinder. Wrap with waxed paper and foil. Refrigerate at least 4 hours. (Can be prepared ahead and refrigerated 3 days or frozen up to 1 month. Thaw dough at room temperature 20 minutes before continuing.)

Preheat oven to 375°F. Line 2 baking sheets with foil or parchment. Cut chilled dough into ⅜ inch slices. Arrange on prepared sheets, spacing 2 inches apart. Refrigerate unsliced dough. Bake cookies until beginning to firm, about 15 minutes. Cool 5 minutes on sheets, then transfer to rack. Repeat with remaining dough. Store cookies in airtight container. Makes about 40.

GIANT FUDGIES

A favorite of big and little chocolate lovers!

½ c. butter, softened
¾ c. granulated sugar
1 large egg
1 tsp. vanilla
1 c. all-purpose flour
½ c. unsweetened cocoa powder

½ tsp. baking soda
1 (6 oz.) can pecans, chopped (about 1½ c.)
1 (6 oz.) pkg. semi-sweet chocolate chips

Heat oven to 375°F. In large bowl with electric mixer at medium speed, beat butter, sugar, egg, vanilla, flour, cocoa powder, and baking soda until thoroughly blended and smooth. Stir in pecans and chocolate chips. Drop dough by ¼ cupfuls onto ungreased large cookie sheet, spacing about 2 inches apart. Using hands, flatten dough into 3½ inch rounds. Bake 10 minutes until dry to touch but still soft. Let cookies cool on cookie sheets 2 minutes. Using metal spatula, remove to wire racks to cool completely. Makes about 10 cookies.

CHOCOLATE CHUNK COOKIES

Indulge yourself with these chunky chocolate cookies!

½ c. butter (room temperature)
½ c. sugar
¼ c. firmly packed brown sugar
1 tsp. vanilla
1 egg
1 c. all-purpose flour
½ tsp. baking soda

½ tsp. salt
2 (4 oz.) pkg. sweet chocolate or 1 (8 oz.) pkg. semi-sweet chocolate, cut into large ⅜ inch chunks*
1⅓ c. flaked coconut (optional)

Beat butter, sugars, vanilla, and egg until light and fluffy. Mix flour with soda and salt; blend into butter mixture. Stir in chocolate chunks and the coconut. Chill 1 hour. Drop 2 inches apart by heaping tablespoon onto ungreased baking sheet. Bake at 350° for 12 to 15 minutes or until lightly browned. Cookies will be soft in center when done. Cool 2 minutes before removing from sheet. Makes 2 dozen (3½ inch) cookies.

* If desired, place an additional 4 ounces sweet chocolate or semi-sweet chocolate chunks on tops of cookies before baking.

CHOCOLATE-CHOCOLATE BROWNIES

This recipe doubles the chocolate.

1 (4 oz.) milk chocolate bar
¾ c. all-purpose flour
¾ c. sugar
6 Tbsp. cocoa

8 Tbsp. butter
2 tsp. vanilla
3 eggs
1 c. walnuts

1. Preheat oven to 325°F. Grease and flour 9x9 inch baking pan.

2. Separate milk chocolate bar into sections. In food processor with metal blade; process chocolate and flour until very coarsely chopped. (Do not overprocess.) Pour into bowl.

3. In food processor with metal blade, process sugar, cocoa, and ¼ teaspoon salt until blended. Cut butter into eight pieces; process 45 seconds. Scrape work bowl; process 15 seconds or until fluffy. Add vanilla and eggs; process 25 seconds. Scrape work bowl; process 5 seconds.

4. Add chocolate-flour mixture and walnuts; process 3 to 5 seconds until nuts are very coarsely chopped.

5. Spoon into pan. Bake for 25 to 30 minutes until toothpick inserted in brownies comes out clean. Cool in pan on wire rack. Cut into 16 pieces. Makes 16 servings.

HOLIDAY CHOCOLATE CHIP SQUARES

A delightful Christmas sweet topped with a cherry.

2¼ c. all-purpose flour
1¼ tsp. baking powder
¼ tsp. salt
1 c. butter, softened
1¼ c. sugar
1 egg
1 tsp. vanilla

1 (12 oz.) pkg. (2 c.) semi-sweet
    chocolate morsels
1 c. chopped nuts
3 (6 oz.) jars (30) maraschino
    cherries, drained, pat dry
16 small candy spearmint leaves,
    cut into quarters lengthwise

Preheat oven to 350°F. In bowl, combine flour, baking powder, and salt; set aside. In bowl, combine butter and sugar; beat until creamy. Add egg and vanilla; mix well. Gradually blend in flour mixture. Stir in semi-sweet chocolate morsels and nuts. Spread into greased 13x9 inch glass baking dish. Press 30 maraschino cherries into dough spacing them to form 6 rows, 5 cherries per row. Place 2 quartered spearmint leaves at base of each cherry; press into dough. Bake at 350°F. for 25 to 30 minutes. Cool. Cut into 2 inch squares. Makes 30 squares.

PEANUT BUTTER CHIP CHOCOLATE COOKIES

A children's favorite.

1 c. butter
1½ c. sugar
2 eggs
2 tsp. vanilla
2 c. unsifted all-purpose flour

⅔ c. cocoa
¾ tsp. baking soda
½ tsp. salt
2 c. (12 oz. pkg.) peanut butter chips

Cream butter, sugar, eggs, and vanilla until light and fluffy. Combine flour, cocoa, baking soda, and salt; add to creamed mixture. Stir in peanut butter chips. Drop by teaspoonfuls onto ungreased cookie sheet. Or, chill until firm enough to handle and shape small amounts of dough into 1 inch balls. Place on ungreased cookie sheet and flatten slightly with fork. Bake at 350° for 8 to 10 minutes. Cool 1 minute before removing from cookie sheet onto wire rack. Makes about 5 dozen (2½ inch) cookies.

CHOCOLATE PEANUT BUTTER BARS

A favorite all time cookie recipe.

1 (6 oz.) pkg. semi-sweet chocolate
½ c. butter, softened
⅔ c. peanut butter
1 c. firmly packed brown sugar
1 egg
1 tsp. vanilla

1¼ c. all-purpose flour
½ tsp. baking soda
½ tsp. salt
1½ c. quick cooking oats (uncooked)

Melt chocolate in top of a double boiler over hot water; set aside. Cream butter and peanut butter. Add sugar, egg, and vanilla, mixing well. Combine flour, soda, and salt; stir into creamed mixture. Stir in oats.

Press three-fourths of peanut butter mixture into a greased 13x9x2 inch baking pan. Spread chocolate over top. Crumble remaining peanut butter mixture over chocolate. Bake at 350° for 18 to 20 minutes. Cool and cut into bars. Makes 2 dozen.

OLD-FASHIONED BROWNIES

Another delicious brownie recipe!

3 (1 oz.) sq. unsweetened chocolate
½ c. shortening
3 eggs
1½ c. granulated sugar

1½ tsp. vanilla
¼ tsp. salt
1 c. all-purpose flour
1½ c. coarsely chopped walnuts

Melt together chocolate and shortening over warm water; cool slightly. Mix together eggs, sugar, vanilla, and salt; blend in chocolate mixture, then flour. Fold in walnuts. Turn into a well greased 8 inch square pan. Bake at 325°F. for about 35 minutes. (Brownies should still be soft.) Cut into 20 bars.

CHOCOLATE DATE ENVELOPES

A luscious chocolate cookie with an added touch of orange.

Cookie:

1¼ c. all-purpose flour
1 (3 oz.) pkg. cream cheese, softened

½ c. butter, softened

Filling:

½ (12 oz.) pkg. (1 c.) Little Bits semi-sweet chocolate
1 (8 oz.) pkg. pitted dates, chopped
½ c. finely chopped walnuts

2 tsp. grated orange rind
2 tsp. orange juice
Confectioners sugar

Cookie: In bowl, combine flour, cream cheese, and butter; knead until well blended. Shape into ball; wrap and refrigerate.

Filling: In bowl, combine Little Bits semi-sweet chocolate, dates, walnuts, orange rind, and juice. Press into ball. Preheat oven to 350°F. On floured board, roll dough into 13 inch square; cut into 2½ inch squares. Shape rounded teaspoonful filling into log. Place in center of square. Bring two diagonal corners of each square to the center and pinch. Place on ungreased cookie sheet. Bake at 350°F. for 20 minutes. Cool. Sprinkle confectioners sugar. Makes 25 envelope cookies.

FIDOS

Another fine holiday cookie. Chocolate of course!

⅔ c. butter, softened
½ c. granulated sugar
1 large egg
1½ c. all-purpose flour
½ c. unsweetened cocoa powder

½ tsp. baking powder
1 egg white, lightly beaten
½ c. finely ground walnuts
Mocha Cream Filling (recipe follows)

Heat oven to 350°F. In large bowl with electric mixer at medium speed, beat butter, sugar, egg, flour, cocoa powder, and baking powder until thoroughly blended and smooth. Roll out half dough at a time to ¼ inch thickness; cut out dough with 3½ inch dog bone cookie cutter or cookie cutters of choice. Arrange cookies on ungreased large cookie sheets, spacing about ½ inch apart. Brush half of cookies lightly with beaten egg white; sprinkle with ground walnuts. Bake all cookies 8 minutes until lightly browned; cool on racks. Meanwhile, prepare Mocha Cream Filling. Spread bottoms of cooled plain cookies with filling; top with decorated cookies. Makes about 18 sandwich cookies.

Mocha Cream Filling: In medium size bowl with electric mixer at medium speed, beat ½ cup butter, softened, until fluffy. Gradually beat in 1 cup confectioners sugar, 3 tablespoons unsweetened cocoa powder, and 1 tablespoon instant coffee powder until blended and smooth.

MOCHA CHOCOLATE CHIP COOKIES

The addition of coffee makes this a delightfully sophisticated cookie.

2¼ c. all-purpose flour
1 tsp. baking soda
½ tsp. salt
1 c. butter (at room temperature)
1¼ c. granulated sugar
¼ c. granulated fructose
2 large eggs
2 tsp. vanilla

¼ c. instant coffee powder (not granules)*
2 (1 oz.) sq. unsweetened chocolate
1 c. (6 oz.) semi-sweet chocolate chips
1¼ c. (5 oz.) chopped walnuts or pecans

Heat oven to 350°. Place chocolate in top of double boiler or heatproof bowl set over barely simmering water. Stir occasionally until melted and smooth; remove from water and let cool. Mix flour, baking soda, and salt. In large bowl, beat butter, sugar, and fructose with electric mixer on medium speed until fluffy. Beat in eggs, vanilla, coffee, and then melted chocolate until blended. With mixer on low speed gradually add flour mixture; beat just until blended. With wooden spoon, stir in chocolate chips and nuts. Scoop dough or drop by heaping tablespoonfuls 2 inches apart onto ungreased cookie sheet. Bake for 10 to 12 minutes until cookies puff and dough loses its shine. Cool on sheet about 1 minute before removing to racks to cool completely. Makes 40.

* Note: You can powder instant coffee granules in a blender or by crushing them with back of a spoon.

MOUSSES, TORTES, AND MORE

CHOCOLATE NUT TORTE

A delicious and fancy chocolate torte, garnished with lovely sugared violets.
Use Sugared Violets (follows).

Torte layers:

7 large eggs
1 c. granulated sugar
1 tsp. vanilla
1¼ c. ground hazelnuts (about 4 oz.)

1¼ c. ground pecans (about 4 oz.)
½ c. packaged dry bread crumbs
1 tsp. baking powder
½ tsp. salt

Filling:

1 c. (½ pt.) heavy (whipping) cream, chilled

¼ c. confectioners sugar
1 tsp. vanilla

Chocolate Buttercream:

1 (8 oz.) pkg. semi-sweet chocolate sq., chopped
¾ lb. (3 sticks) unsalted butter, softened
2 c. sifted confectioners sugar

Dash of salt
3 large egg yolks
¼ c. seedless raspberry jam (optional)

1. Day before: Make Sugared Violets; let dry overnight.

2. Make torte layers; separate eggs, placing whites in large bowl of electric mixer and yolks in smaller bowl. Let whites warm to room temperature for 20 minutes.

3. Preheat oven to 375°F. Line bottom of three 9 inch round layer cake pans with circles of waxed paper. With mixer at high speed, beat egg whites until soft peaks form when beater is slowly raised. Gradually beat in ½ cup granulated sugar, beating until stiff peaks form. With same beater, beat egg yolks with remaining ½ cup granulated sugar until thick and light, about 3 minutes; beat in 1 teaspoon vanilla.

4. On waxed paper, combine ground nuts, bread crumbs, baking powder, and ½ teaspoon salt. Add to yolk mixture; stir to mix. Add one-third of beaten white mixture to yolk mixture, stirring until blended. With rubber spatula, fold yolk mixture into white mixture until no white streaks remain. Pour into prepared pans, dividing evenly; smooth surfaces. Bake 20 minutes, or until surface is lightly browned and springs back when gently touched. To cool, invert and set pans on wire racks. Cool cakes completely in pans, about 1 hour.

5. Meanwhile, make filling: In small bowl of electric mixer, beat cream with ¼ cup of confectioners sugar and the vanilla until stiff peaks form; spoon into another small bowl. Refrigerate.

6. Make Chocolate Buttercream: In top of double boiler, over hot, not boiling, water, melt chocolate, stirring occasionally; remove from heat. (Or, place chocolate

in glass bowl; microwave on HIGH until melted, 2 minutes, stirring after each minute.) Cool completely.

7. In small bowl of electric mixer, beat butter until light and fluffy. Add cooled chocolate and gradually beat in confectioners sugar and salt. Add egg yolks, one at a time, beating well after each addition.

8. To assemble cake: Run small-bladed knife around side of each pan to loosen cake layers. Invert and tap each pan to release cake layers. Peel off and discard wax paper. Place one cake layer on serving plate. With flat icing spatula, spread half of raspberry jam evenly on layer. Spoon half of filling onto cake layer; spread evenly. Place second cake layer on first; spread remaining jam and filling on layer. Place remaining layer on top. If necessary, use serrated knife to trim uneven side of cake.

9. Spoon one-third of Buttercream into pastry bag fitted with ¼ inch star tip; set aside. With icing spatula, spread remaining two-thirds of Buttercream to cover side and top of cake, running spatula over Buttercream to smooth surface. Pipe a shell border around bottom and top edges of cake. With tip of knife, lightly mark top edge of side of cake at eight even intervals. Beginning at top edge, pipe a shell swag onto side of cake from one mark to the next. Repeat to make eight swags. To garnish, press a Sugared Violet into icing at each junction of swags. Place additional violets and violet leaves around cake if desired. Makes 16 servings.

Sugared Violets - (Sugared Violets should be made day ahead to allow for drying):

Fresh violets in assorted colors*   **Granulated sugar**
1 egg white, slightly beaten

1. Cut each violet with a 1 inch long stem just before sugaring. Dip small craft paintbrush into egg white and brush underside, then top side of petals until coated. Using small spoon, holding violet over bowl, lightly sprinkle both sides of petals with sugar, shaking off excess and reserving sugar in bowl to use again.

2. Set Sugared Violets on wire rack placed over waxed paper covered tray to dry. When violets are completely dried, store in single layer in airtight container (Sugared Violets will keep indefinitely if properly stored).

* Note: Many nontoxic flowers, such as pansies, cosmos, and wild roses, can be substituted for violets. Select flowers with only a few petals, since they are easier to coat and dry. (Flowers from florists may have been sprayed with insecticide and should not be eaten.)

CHOCOLATE MOUSSE CHARLOTTE

A very fancy chocolate dessert, a chocolate classic.

5 large eggs
1 (12 oz.) pkg. semi-sweet
    chocolate pieces
½ c. (1 stick) unsalted butter
¼ c. unsweetened cocoa

3 Tbsp. orange flavored liqueur or
    orange juice
2 (3 oz.) pkg. ladyfingers
¼ c. sugar

1. Separate eggs, placing the whites in large bowl of mixer; let warm to room temperature. Place yolks in a small bowl and set aside.

2. In top of double boiler, over hot, not boiling water, melt chocolate and butter. (Or, place chocolate and butter in microwave-safe, medium bowl; microwave at HIGH 2 to 3 minutes, stirring once or twice.) With spoon, mix in cocoa and liqueur. Stir in egg yolks, one at a time, until blended; set aside.

3. Using a large piece of heavy-duty foil, line a straight-sided 2½ quart casserole or souffle dish, extending foil over rim by an inch. (Foil helps to lift Charlotte from casserole when removing to serving platter.) Press foil smoothly into dish. Keeping ladyfingers attached, separate one package to make four layers. Arrange three layers around side of dish, rounded sides against dish. Separate and reserve 14 ladyfinger pieces from other package; press all remaining pieces into bottom of dish, crumbling some to fill cracks between the upright ladyfingers.

4. When chocolate mixture has cooled, with electric mixer at high speed, beat egg whites until foamy. Gradually beat in sugar; continue to beat until stiff peaks form when beater is slowly raised.

5. With rubber spatula, gently fold chocolate mixture into egg whites, using an under-and-over motion. Fold only enough to combine - there should be no white streaks. Pour half into prepared dish; layer 8 of the reserved ladyfingers on mixture; cover with remaining mixture. Cut remaining 6 ladyfingers lengthwise diagonally in half. Arrange rounded sides up and pointed ends to center, on top of mousse mixture. Cover with plastic wrap; freeze until firm.

6. Several hours before serving, using foil overhang, lift from dish. Remove and discard foil. Place Charlotte on serving plate. Refrigerate at least 1½ hours before serving. Makes 12 servings.

Note: This dessert can be made up to a week ahead.

CHOCOLATE MOUSSE CAKE

A cake and a mousse too!

1 c. chocolate wafer crumbs (about 20 cookies)
Butter
3 (12 oz.) pkg. semi-sweet chocolate pieces
5 eggs, separated (at room temperature)

2 tsp. instant coffee powder
⅓ c. orange flavor liqueur
2 c. heavy or whipping cream
Confectioners sugar
Chocolate Ruffles (follows)
Chocolate Glaze (follows)

Day ahead:

1. In 10x3 inch springform pan, mix chocolate wafer crumbs and 4 tablespoons softened butter. Press mixture onto bottom of pan; refrigerate.

2. Cut ¾ cup butter (1½ sticks) into small pieces. In heavy 4 quart saucepan over low heat, heat cut up butter and chocolate pieces until butter and chocolate just melt and mixture is smooth, stirring constantly. Remove saucepan from heat.

3. In medium bowl, with wire whisk, beat egg yolks and instant coffee powder until coffee dissolves; beat egg yolk mixture into melted chocolate mixture, then slowly beat in orange flavor liqueur.

4. In large bowl with mixer at medium speed, beat heavy or whipping cream until stiff peaks form. Fold whipped cream, half at a time, into chocolate mixture.

5. In small bowl with mixer at high speed, beat egg whites until foamy. Add ¼ cup confectioners sugar and continue beating until whites stand in stiff peaks. With rubber spatula, fold beaten whites, half at a time, into chocolate mixture until blended. Pour mixture over crust in springform pan. Cover and refrigerate overnight.

6. Prepare Chocolate Ruffles; refrigerate.

Next day:

7. Prepare Chocolate Glaze. Remove side of springform pan from cake. Place cake, still on pan bottom, on wire rack over waxed paper. Spread Chocolate Glaze over top and down side of cake. Refrigerate.

8. To serve, place cake on cake plate. Arrange Chocolate Ruffles in concentric circles on top of cake; sprinkle with confectioners sugar. Makes 32 servings.

Chocolate Ruffles: In heavy 1 quart saucepan over low heat, heat one 8 ounce package semi-sweet chocolate squares, chopped, until chocolate melts, stirring constantly. Spoon about ¼ cup melted chocolate onto inverted 15½ x 10½ inch jelly roll pan. With metal spatula, spread chocolate to cover pan bottom evenly. Refrigerate just until chocolate is firm, about 10 minutes.

Make Ruffles: Place chocolate covered jelly roll pan, with 10½ inch side toward you, on damp cloth to keep it from moving while working. With blade of metal spatula or side of small pancake turner, starting at the far right corner, scrape up about 3 inch wide strip chocolate toward you, pulling spatula with right hand, gathering left side of chocolate strip with left hand, and allowing right side to fan out. (Consistency of chocolate if very important. If it is too soft, it will gather into a mush; if too hard, it will break and crumble. If chocolate is too firm, let stand at room temperature a few minutes until soft enough to work with; if too soft, return to refrigerator.) Place ruffles on cookie sheet; refrigerate until firm. Continue making 3 inch wide ruffles with chocolate on jelly roll pan. Repeat with remaining melted chocolate, using a clean jelly roll pan each time. (The more jelly roll pans you have the faster you can make the ruffles.) If ruffles break while making, return chocolate to saucepan and melt again, heating only until melted or chocolate will not make ruffles properly.

Chocolate Glaze: In 2 quart saucepan over low heat, heat three-fourths 12 ounce package semi-sweet chocolate pieces (1½ cups), 2 tablespoons confectioners sugar, 3 tablespoons orange flavor liqueur, 3 tablespoons milk, and 1 teaspoon instant coffee powder until chocolate melts and mixture is smooth, stirring. Remove saucepan from heat. Let glaze stand at room temperature to cool slightly until of good spreading consistency. Makes about 2 cups.

CHOCOLATE COOKIE TORTE

Fun to make and delightful to eat!

1½ c. butter, softened
2 c. granulated sugar
2 large eggs
2 c. all-purpose flour
⅔ c. unsweetened cocoa powder
1 Tbsp. ground cinnamon, plus
  additional for garnish

1 c. whipped and sweetened cream
Cinnamon sticks (optional)
Heart shaped chocolate candies
  (optional)

Heat oven to 375°F. Tear off 7 sheets of wax paper, each about 10 inches long. On one sheet trace around 9 inch round cake pan. Stack sheets of wax paper, with traced pattern on top; cut out circles. Arrange circles on large cookie sheets, two to a sheet;* set aside. In large bowl with electric mixer at medium speed, beat butter, sugar, eggs, flour, cocoa powder, and 1 tablespoon cinnamon until well blended. Spread mixture evenly over wax paper circles, leaving about ½ inch margin around edges; bake, two cookie sheets at a time, 8 minutes until cookies are dry to touch but still soft. Let cool 2 minutes; carefully peel off paper. Let cool completely on wire racks.

To assemble torte: Place one cookie on serving plate; spread with about ½ cup whipped cream, piping a decorative edge around outside of cookie. Repeat layering with remaining cookies and whipped cream, piping in decorative patter over top of cookie. Sprinkle with cinnamon; garnish center of torte with cinnamon sticks and heart shaped chocolate candies if desired. Makes 10 servings.

* Note: If you have only one or two large cookie sheets prepare and bake cookies in batches, letting cookie sheet or sheets cool between batches.

SURPRISE WAFFLES WITH RASPBERRY SAUCE

The batter also makes good pancakes - figure about ½ cup for each. For a quick version of this recipe, forget the batter and sprinkle packaged frozen waffles with chocolate chips, then heat in regular or toaster oven.

Raspberry Sauce (recipe follows)
3 large eggs
¾ c. sour cream
¾ c. milk
1¼ c. all-purpose flour
2 tsp. baking powder
½ tsp. baking soda

¼ tsp. salt
1 tsp. vanilla
⅓ c. butter, melted
⅓ c. semi-sweet chocolate chips
1 c. whipping cream, whipped stiff
  with 2 Tbsp. sugar

Make Raspberry Sauce. Beat eggs, sour cream, and milk in medium size bowl with wire whisk or fork until smooth. Add flour, baking powder, baking soda, salt, and vanilla; beat just until smooth. Stir in butter until blended. Pour batter onto waffle iron, preferably with nonstick coating. (You'll need a scant ¾ cup for an 8 inch waffle.) Sprinkle about 1 tablespoon chocolate chips evenly over each waffle before baking to a golden brown. Cool waffles on racks. Meanwhile, gently reheat Raspberry Sauce. Cut waffles in quarters. For each serving, stack 5 quarters with whipped cream between layers. Top with a dollop whipped cream and warm sauce. Serve immediately. Makes 4 servings.

Raspberry Sauce: Puree 1 (10 ounce) package thawed frozen raspberries in blender or food processor. Pour through a fine strainer into small saucepan. Add 1 tablespoon granulated sugar and mixture of 2 teaspoons cornstarch and 2 tablespoons water. Stir over medium heat until boiling, slightly thickened, and transparent. Remove from heat. Makes 1 cup.

SWEET DREAM TORTE

Easy to prepare and especially good, too.

1 (8 oz.) pkg. cream cheese, softened
1¼ c. sifted confectioners sugar
½ tsp. vanilla
1 (1 oz.) sq. unsweetened chocolate, melted

¾ c. whipping cream
1 (10¾ oz.) frozen pound cake, thawed

Combine cream cheese, 1 cup sugar, and vanilla, mixing until well blended. Blend in chocolate. Beat cream until soft peaks form; gradually add remaining sugar, beating until stiff peaks form. Fold into cream cheese mixture. Split cake into three layers. Spread each layer with cream cheese mixture; stack. Frost sides with cream cheese mixture. Chill. Makes 8 to 10 servings.

CAROB MOUSSE

Another delicious dessert made with carob, a chocolate substitute.

1 lb. Ricotta cheese
1 Tbsp. carob powder
1 tsp. instant decaffeinated coffee powder

¼ c. milk
2 Tbsp. honey
1 Tbsp. Amaretto liqueur

Combine Ricotta, carob, coffee, milk, honey, and Amaretto in a medium size bowl; beat with an electric mixer until well blended. Cover and refrigerate until serving time. Serves 6.

FUDGE CREAM HEARTS

A delightful combination, chocolate and hearts.

6 (6 inch) sq. cheesecloth
1 (8 oz.) pkg. cream cheese, cut up
2 Tbsp. bottled fudge sauce

¼ c. sifted confectioners sugar
1 c. whipping cream

Moisten the cheesecloth squares. Line six ½ cup molds or custard cups with the cheesecloth, overlapping edges. Beat the cheese and fudge sauce with an electric mixer till well combined. Add sugar; beat on high speed till fluffy.

Wash beaters. In another bowl, beat cream till soft peaks form; fold into fudge mixture. Spoon into molds. Cover with cheesecloth; quick-chill in freezer 30 to 45 minutes or chill in refrigerator 3 to 24 hours. To serve, spoon additional fudge sauce onto serving plates. Unmold; remove cheesecloth. Place on plates; top with purchased chocolates. Drizzle with sauce. Serves 6.

CHOCOLATE FLOATING ISLANDS

A very special and pretty chocolate dessert.

2 egg whites	**2 eggs**
¼ tsp. cream of tartar	**1 tsp. vanilla**
¼ c. sugar	**1 (1 oz.) sq. unsweetened**
3 c. milk	**chocolate, melted**
½ c. semi-sweet chocolate pieces	**1 tsp. shortening, melted**
½ c. sugar	**2 Tbsp. chopped pistachio nuts**
2 egg yolks	

In mixer bowl, beat egg whites and cream of tartar till soft peaks form (tips curl over). Gradually add the ¼ cup sugar, beating to stiff peaks (tips straight). In a 10 inch skillet, heat milk till *barely* simmering. Divide meringue mixture into 6 equal portions; drop each into milk. Simmer, uncovered, 5 minutes or till firm. Lift meringues from milk with slotted spoon and drain on paper toweling. Chill.

Add the chocolate pieces to milk in skillet. Heat and stir till chocolate melts. Stir in the ½ cup sugar. Beat egg yolks and whole eggs; gradually and carefully stir chocolate mixture into eggs. Transfer to a 2 quart saucepan. Cook and stir over medium heat till mixture coats a metal spoon. Remove from heat; cool quickly by setting saucepan in a bowl of ice water. Stir in vanilla; continue stirring gently for 1 to 2 minutes to hasten cooling. Turn into serving bowl. Chill thoroughly.

To serve, arrange meringues atop chocolate custard. Combine melted chocolate and shortening. Drizzle over meringues. Sprinkle with pistachio nuts. Makes 6 servings.

TIRAMISU

This Italian dessert, a must on the most fashionable restaurant menus, is made with layers of ladyfingers soaked in espresso and coffee liqueur, mascarpone cheese, and topped with chocolate shavings.

1 (16 oz.) container mascarpone cheese*	**1½ c. heavy or whipping cream**
	2 tsp. instant espresso coffee
Confectioners sugar	**powder**
Coffee flavor liqueur	**2 (3 to 4½ oz.) pkg. ladyfingers**
Vanilla	
3 sq. semi-sweet chocolate, coarsely grated	

About 3 hours before serving or early in day:

1. In large bowl, with wire whisk or fork, beat mascarpone, ½ cup confectioners sugar, 3 tablespoons coffee flavor liqueur, 1 teaspoon vanilla, two-thirds of grated chocolate, and ½ teaspoon salt. (Set aside remaining chocolate for top of dessert.)

2. In small bowl, with mixer at medium speed, beat 1 cup heavy or whipping cream until soft peaks form. With rubber spatula or wire whisk, fold whipped cream into cheese mixture.

3. In small bowl, stir instant espresso powder, ⅓ cup coffee flavor liqueur, ½ teaspoon vanilla, and 2 tablespoons water.

4. Separate ladyfingers into halves. Line 10 cup glass or crystal bowl with one-fourth of ladyfingers; brush with 2 tablespoons of espresso mixture. Spoon one-third of cheese mixture over ladyfingers. Repeat with ladyfingers, espresso mixture, and cheese mixture to make 2 more layers. Top with remaining ladyfingers, gently pressing ladyfingers into cheese mixture. Brush ladyfingers with remaining espresso mixture. Sprinkle remaining grated chocolate over top of dessert, reserving 1 tablespoon for garnish.

5. In small bowl, with mixer at medium speed, beat remaining ½ cup heavy or whipping cream and 2 tablespoons confectioners sugar until soft peaks form. Spoon whipped cream mixture into decorating bag with large star tube. Pipe large rosettes on top of dessert. Sprinkle reserved grated chocolate on rosettes. Cover dessert and refrigerate at least 2 hours to chill and blend flavors. Makes 16 servings.

* If mascarpone cheese in not available, substitute two 8 ounce packages cream cheese, softened, and in step 1 in large bowl, with mixer at medium speed, beat cream cheese and 3 tablespoons milk until smooth and fluffy. Increase confectioners sugar to ⅔ cup and beat in with coffee flavor liqueur and vanilla. Stir in grated chocolate; delete salt.

CHOCOLATE CUPS WITH BANANA FILLING

You can make the chocolate cups ahead and refrigerate in a covered container until ready to fill.

6 small (3 oz.) paper cups
1 c. (6 oz.) semi-sweet chocolate chips, melted and stirred smooth
½ c. whipping cream
1 Tbsp. granulated sugar
1 tsp. unsweetened cocoa powder or ½ tsp. instant espresso granules

1 medium size firm, ripe banana, coarsely chopped
2 Tbsp. semi-sweet chocolate mini chips
2 (3 x ¼ inch) strips orange peel (optional)

Spray inside of paper cups lightly with vegetable cooking spray. Place 1 rounded measuring tablespoon melted chocolate into 1 cup. Tilting cup, spread chocolate with small spatula until bottom and sides are evenly coated to within ¼ inch of rim. Repeat with remaining cups. Chill in freezer or refrigerator at least 1 hour or until firm. Holding cup in one hand and small paring knife in other, cut slit in rim of paper cup; peel off paper around sides, using a circular motion. Carefully peel off bottom Return chocolate cups to freezer or refrigerator. Just before serving, beat cream, sugar, and cocoa in a small bowl with electric mixer until soft peaks form when beaters are lifted. Fold in bananas. Spoon into chocolate cups; sprinkle with chocolate chips. Tuck ends of 1 strip orange peel into each cup at sides as a "handle." Serve immediately. Makes 6 servings.

CHOCOLATE NECTARINE SHORTCAKE

Choose bright-looking nectarines that are firm and rounded. To serve this luscious shortcake warm, just bake it the day of the party.

1⅔ c. all-purpose flour
⅓ c. unsweetened cocoa powder
½ c. sugar
2 tsp. baking powder
¼ tsp. baking soda
½ c. butter
1 beaten egg
⅔ c. milk

6 medium nectarines, pitted and
   sliced (4 c.)
¼ c. sugar
1 c. whipping cream
2 Tbsp. sugar
½ tsp. vanilla
Whipped cream

In a mixing bowl, stir together the flour, cocoa powder, ½ cup sugar, baking powder, and soda. Cut in the butter till mixture resembles coarse crumbs. Combine the egg and milk; add all at once to the dry ingredients and stir just to moisten.

Spread shortcake dough into a greased 5 cup ovenproof ring mold or 9 x 1½ inch round cake pan. Bake in a 450° oven for 15 to 18 minutes for ring mold or cake pan or till done. Cool 10 minutes on wire rack. Remove from pan; place shortcake on serving plate. Cover and store at room temperature.

Combine the nectarines and ¼ cup sugar; set aside. Beat whipping cream, 2 tablespoons sugar, and vanilla with an electric mixer on medium speed or rotary beater till soft peaks form. Place sliced nectarines in a bowl in the center of the shortcake. Serve warm or cooled with whipped cream. Makes 8 servings.

POACHED LEMON-CHOCOLATE PEARS

A new version of the classic combination.

1 c. dry white wine or water
⅓ c. granulated sugar
2 (2x1 inch) strips lemon peel
2 Tbsp. lemon peel

6 large firm pears (about 3 lb.),
   peeled and cored
3 Tbsp. semi-sweet chocolate chips

In a saucepan wide and deep enough to hold the pears upright, bring wine, sugar, lemon peel, and juice to a boil. Add pears; return to a boil. Reduce heat; cover and simmer 20 minutes or until pears are tender when pierced with a pick. Remove with slotted spoon to serving dish. Boil cooking liquid over high heat about 5 minutes until syrupy. Pour over pears. Press a few chocolate chips flat sides in against each pear. The chips will melt slightly. Serve warm or at room temperature. Makes 6 servings.

STRAWBERRY ALMOND DACQUOISE

A delightful dinner party dessert, chocolate filled.

6 egg whites, separated (at room temperature)
¼ tsp. cream of tartar
1 c. sugar
½ c. slivered blanched almonds, toasted and finely ground

2 pt. strawberries
Chocolate Butter-Cream Filling
½ c. heavy or whipping cream

Early in day:

1. Line 2 large cookie sheets with foil. With toothpick, outline two 8 inch circles on each cookie sheet.

2. In bowl with mixer at high speed, beat egg whites and cream of tartar to soft peaks. Beat in sugar, 2 tablespoons at a time, until dissolved and whites stand in stiff, glossy peaks. Fold in almonds.

3. Preheat oven to 275°F. Spread meringue inside circles. Bake 1 hour or until golden brown. Cool 10 minutes; loosen from cookie sheets and remove to wire racks to cool.

4. Slice enough strawberries to make ¾ cup. Prepare Chocolate Butter-Cream Filling.

5. Place 1 meringue layer on plate; spread with ⅓ of butter cream. Top with ⅓ of sliced strawberries. Repeat to make 2 more layers. Top with last meringue layer.

6. In bowl with mixer at medium speed, beat cream to stiff peaks. Spoon 1⅓ cups whipped cream into decorating bag with large star tube; set aside. Spread remaining whipped cream on side of cake. With cream in decorating bag, decorate top edge of cake. Refrigerate 4 hours to soften meringue layers slightly for easier cutting.

7. To serve, cut each of the remaining strawberries in halves. Press 16 strawberry halves into cream on side of cake. Pile remaining strawberry halves on center of cake. Makes 16 servings.

Chocolate Butter-Cream Filling: In bowl with mixer at low speed, beat 1½ cups confectioners sugar and ¾ cup butter (1½ sticks), softened, until just mixed. At high speed, beat until fluffy. At medium speed, gradually beat in 2 egg yolks, 2 squares unsweetened chocolate, melted and cooled, and ½ teaspoon vanilla until smooth. Makes about 2½ cups.

CHOCOLATE MOUSSE

A delectable dessert. Coffee flavored.

4 egg yolks
¾ c. sugar
¼ c. Grand Marnier
6 oz. semi-sweet chocolate (in chunks)

4 Tbsp. brewed black coffee
6 oz. butter
4 egg whites
2 Tbsp. confectioners sugar

Combine egg yolks, sugar, and Grand Marnier in a double boiler and heat until sugar melted thoroughly. In a separate pan, melt chocolate and coffee together and add butter a little at a time. Mix thoroughly. Beat egg whites until stiff, then slowly add confectioners sugar while continuing to beat. Combine egg yolk and chocolate mixtures and fold quickly into whites. Mix thoroughly and pour into individual serving dishes. Chill immediately. Serves 4 to 6.

COCOA-RUM PUDDING

Your guests with love this warm treat with mouth watering hard sauce melting over the top.

2 c. French bread cubes
2 c. milk
1 c. sugar
½ c. unsweetened cocoa powder
½ tsp. ground cinnamon

2 slightly beaten eggs
½ c. raisins
1 Tbsp. butter, melted
2 tsp. vanilla

Place bread cubes in a large bowl; add milk and let stand about 10 minutes. In a small bowl, stir together sugar, cocoa powder, and cinnamon. Combine eggs, raisins, butter or margarine, and vanilla; add sugar mixture and mix well. Stir into bread. Pour bread mixture into an ungreased 10x6x2 inch baking dish. Bake in a 375° oven for 40 to 45 minutes or till knife inserted near center comes out clean. Serve warm with Sweet Rum Hard Sauce. Makes 6 to 8 servings.

Sweet Rum Hard Sauce: In a small mixer bowl, beat together ½ cup butter or margarine and 1 cup sifted powdered sugar. Add 1 tablespoon rum or ½ teaspoon rum extract; beat till fluffy. Cover and chill. Makes ¾ cup.

MOCHA-FILLED CHOCOLATE CONES

Just lovely to serve at a dinner party.

4 (1 oz.) sq. semi-sweet chocolate
2 tsp. butter
1 c. heavy cream
2 tsp. unsweetened cocoa powder
2 tsp. instant espresso coffee powder

2 Tbsp. coffee flavored liqueur or strong brewed coffee
2 Tbsp. grated semi-sweet chocolate
Thin orange slices (optional)

In small heavy saucepan over very low heat, melt chocolate and butter, stirring frequently until blended and smooth. On large sheet of wax paper, trace eight 4 inch circles. Spread melted chocolate mixture in thin layer on circles. Refrigerate about 5 minutes until pliable and easy to shape, but not firm or brittle. Meanwhile, in large bowl with electric mixer at high speed, beat cream, cocoa powder, and coffee powder until soft peaks form; beat in liqueur until cream is stiff. When chocolate is ready shape circles into cones, gently peeling away paper and pressing ends of cones together to hold shape. Fit pastry bag with rosette tip; fill bag with mocha cream. Pipe cream into cones. Garnish with grated chocolate. Refrigerate until ready to serve. Serve with orange slices if desired. Makes 8 servings.

BLACK FOREST PARFAITS

An extra special chocolate dessert.

½ c. mini chocolate chips
1 (8 oz.) container Ricotta cheese
1 (3 oz.) pkg. cream cheese,
    softened
2 Tbsp. confectioners sugar

1 (21 oz.) can cherry pie filling
¼ c. heavy cream, whipped
4 heart shaped chocolate candies
    (optional)

Set 2 teaspoons mini chocolate chips aside for garnish; in small saucepan over very low heat, melt remaining chocolate chips, stirring frequently until smooth. Remove from heat; cool slightly. In blender or food processor, blend Ricotta cheese, cream cheese, confectioners sugar, and melted chocolate until smooth. Divide half of chocolate mixture evenly among four 6 ounce dessert dishes or parfait glasses. Using fork, remove cherries from pie filling; reserve ¼ cup thick cherry syrup. Press cherries into chocolate mixture in glasses, dividing evenly; spoon remaining chocolate mixture over cherries. Garnish each serving with 2 tablespoons whipped cream, a spoonful of reserving cherry syrup, a few reserved mini chocolate chips, and one heart shaped chocolate candy if desired. Makes 4 servings.

CONFECTIONS, FUDGES, AND FONDUE

CHOCOLATE-RUM CONFECTIONS

Make lots for the holidays.

8 (1 oz.) sq. semi-sweet chocolate
1 c. confectioners sugar, lightly
   spooned into cup
1 egg
½ c. golden raisins

1 Tbsp. dark rum or thawed
   undiluted orange juice
   concentrate
About ¾ c. finely chopped pecans

In large heavy saucepan over very low heat partially melt chocolate. Remove from heat. Beat with wooden spoon until melted and smooth. Beat in sugar and egg just until smooth. Stir in raisins and rum. Chill mixture until firm enough to handle, 20 to 30 minutes. Using 1 level teaspoon for each, pack firmly in ½ inch balls. (If candy seems dry, moisten hands to shape balls.) Press pecans firmly onto balls. (For easier coating, first brush balls lightly with corn syrup, beaten egg white, or water, then coat with pecans.) Store airtight in cool, dry place. Makes about 60.

CHOCOLATE CITRUS PEELS

Serve with coffee at the end of a rich meal or as a sweet nibble during the holiday season.

3 grapefruit
3 navel oranges
4½ c. sugar

1 c. water
3 (1 oz.) sq. semi-sweet chocolate

Cut each grapefruit and orange in halves. Remove the fruit sections or squeeze out the juice, reserving for other uses. Cut peels into ½ inch wide strips; make strips as uniform and even as possible. Remove white pith from back of skin with paring knife. Place peels in saucepan with water to cover. Bring to boiling; boil 5 minutes. Drain. Repeat. This will remove the bitter taste from the peels.

Combine 2 cups of the sugar and the water in a large heavy saucepan. Bring to boiling. Add peels; cook until peels become transparent and all the sugar syrup is absorbed, about 45 minutes. Watch carefully toward the end so you don't scorch the saucepan. Spread remaining 2½ cups sugar on jelly roll pan lined with wax paper. Lift peels with tongs; roll peels in sugar until thoroughly coated. Lay strips, skin side up, on wire racks. Cover loosely with wax paper. Let dry 2 or 3 days. Makes about 84 pieces.

FOOLPROOF CHOCOLATE FUDGE

The confectioners coating can be bought in candy stores.

3 (6 oz.) pkg. semi-sweet chocolate
   chips
1 (14 oz.) can sweetened
   condensed milk (not
   evaporated milk)

Dash of salt
1½ tsp. vanilla
½ c. chopped pecans (optional)

In heavy saucepan, over low heat, melt chips with condensed milk. Remove from heat; stir in remaining ingredients. Spread evenly into wax paper lined 8 inch square pan. Chill 2 to 3 hours or until firm. Turn fudge onto cutting board; peel off paper and cut into squares. Store loosely covered at room temperature.

White Confetti Fudge: In heavy saucepan, melt 1½ pounds confectioners coating with condensed milk; remove from heat. Stir in ⅛ teaspoon salt, 1 teaspoon vanilla, and 1 cup chopped candied cherries. Proceed as directed. (Makes about 2½ pounds.) Makes about 1¾ pounds.

CHOCOLATE-NUT BRITTLE

This candy is also delicious over ice cream. Break into pieces and serve in the chocolate sauce.

2 c. sugar
1 c. light corn syrup
½ c. water
1 tsp. salt
2 Tbsp. butter

3 (1 oz.) sq. unsweetened chocolate
1 tsp. baking soda
2 tsp. vanilla
2 c. peanuts

In heavy 3 quart saucepan over medium heat, bring to boil sugar, syrup, water, salt, and butter, stirring constantly. Cook *without stirring* to hard crack stage (300° on candy thermometer). Remove from heat. Quickly stir in chocolate, then baking soda, vanilla, and peanuts. Turn into greased 15x10x1 inch jelly roll pan; with greased spatula spread to cover pan. Cool. Turn out of pan onto waxed paper. With mallet, break in irregular pieces. Makes about 2 pounds.

CHOCOLATE CANDY DROPS

Store in pretty candy tins for instant gifts.

2 sticks butter
½ c. peanut butter
1 box confectioners sugar

1¼ c. graham cracker crumbs
1 c. nuts, finely chopped
1 c. coconut

Mix all together; make into balls. Melt 12 ounce package chocolate chips with ½ square paraffin and dip balls into chocolate. Makes about 40.

FANTASY FUDGE

Garnish with extra nuts if desired.

3 c. sugar
¾ c. butter
⅔ c. undiluted evaporated milk
1 (12 oz.) pkg. semi-sweet
    chocolate pieces

1 (7 oz.) jar marshmallow creme
1 c. chopped nuts
1 tsp. vanilla

Combine sugar, butter, and milk in heavy 2½ quart saucepan; bring to full rolling boil, stirring constantly. Continue boiling 5 minutes over medium heat, stirring constantly to prevent scorching. Remove from heat; stir in chocolate pieces until melted. Add marshmallow creme, nuts, and vanilla; beat until well blended. Pour into greased 13x9 inch pan. Cool at room temperature; cut into square. Makes approximately 3 pounds.

CHOCOLATE-DIPPED DELIGHTS

Irresistible little chocolate dipped treats.

Assorted fruit (choose from a fresh orange, canned mandarin orange sections, whole maraschino cherries with stems, whole fresh strawberries, fresh or frozen raspberries or blueberries, or dried fruit)

Creamy peanut butter or canned frosting
Graham cracker sq., cut into quarters
½ lb. chocolate flavored confectioners coating, finely chopped

Prepare fruit: Peel and section orange. Place fresh or canned orange sections, cherries, or berries on paper towels; dry 2 hours, turning once. Cut dried fruit into ¼ inch wide strips. Spread peanut butter or frosting between cracker squares. Put coating in top of the double boiler set over the simmering water; stir constantly till melted. Remove from heat; let stand over hot water. Dip the desired morsel as directed in following. Place on baking sheet lined with waxed paper. Let stand till chocolate hardens; peel off waxed paper. Store fresh fruit in the refrigerator; serve within 24 hours.

Dipping directions: Drop orange sections, dried fruit, or cracker sandwiches, one at a time, into melted coating. Use fork to lift out fruit. Avoid piercing fruit; liquid causes the dipping chocolate to lump. Draw fork across rim of pan. Using another fork, gently push morsel onto waxed paper.

To dip cherries or strawberries, hold by the stems; dip to coat a portion or the whole piece of fruit. Allow excess to drip off. For the raspberries or blueberries, place 2 or 3 in paper candy cups; spoon coating over berries to cover. Chill.

CHOCOLATE BRANDY BALLS

These make lovely holiday gifts.

13½ oz. pkg. graham cracker crumbs
1 c. confectioners sugar
¼ c. cocoa
8 oz. finely chopped walnuts

¼ c. corn syrup or liquid brown sugar
⅓ c. orange liqueur
⅓ c. brandy

Blend by hand until pasty, then pinch off pieces to shape ¾ inch balls. Place in Show-It-All containers and chill overnight. Makes 6 dozen.

COCOA SQUARES WITH FUDGE SAUCE

A different fudge candy. Serve with or without the sauce. Use the sauce on pears or ice cream, too.

⅔ c. granulated sugar
⅓ c. vegetable oil
2 large eggs
½ tsp. vanilla
¾ c. all-purpose flour

⅓ c. unsweetened cocoa powder
¼ tsp. baking powder
¼ tsp. salt
Fudge Sauce (recipe follows)

Heat oven to 350°. Grease an 8 inch square baking pan. Mix sugar and oil in a medium size bowl. With fork or wire whisk, beat in eggs, one at a time, beating well after each. Stir in vanilla. Mix flour, cocoa, baking powder, and salt; add to sugar mixture. Beat with spoon until well blended. Turn into prepared pan and bake for 20 minutes or until pick inserted near center comes out clean. Cool in pan on rack. Cut in 16 squares; serve with Fudge Sauce.

Fudge Sauce: Mix ½ cup granulated sugar and ⅓ cup unsweetened cocoa powder in a small saucepan. Stir in ½ cup evaporated milk and ¼ cup light or dark corn syrup. Bring to boil, stirring constantly. Boil 1 minute; remove from heat and stir in ¼ cup butter until melted, then stir in ½ teaspoon vanilla. Serve warm. Makes 1½ cups.

CARAMEL NUT CENTERS

If there are more caramels than you want to dip, wrap any undipped caramels individually in pieces of clear plastic wrap.

½ c. butter
1 c. packed brown sugar
Dash of salt
½ c. light corn syrup

⅔ c. sweetened condensed milk
½ tsp. vanilla
½ c. chopped pecans

Melt butter in heavy 1½ quart saucepan. Add sugar and salt; stir thoroughly. Stir in corn syrup; mix well. Gradually add milk, stirring constantly. Cook and stir over medium heat to soft ball stage (238°). Remove from heat; stir in vanilla and nuts. Pour into buttered 8x8x2 inch baking pan. Cool. Cut into 1 x ¾ inch rectangles. Shape each into a 1¼ x ½ x ½ inch log. Dip in melted chocolate or almond bark. Makes 8 dozen.

DATE-PEANUT BUTTER CENTERS

Make a variety of chocolate dipped candy for the holidays.

½ c. chunk style peanut butter
1 Tbsp. butter, softened
½ c. sifted confectioners sugar

½ c. pitted whole dates, finely chopped

Stir together peanut butter and butter. Add confectioners sugar and dates; mix well. Shape into ½ inch squares. Dip in melted chocolate or almond bark. Makes 3½ to 4 dozen.

FRUIT BALLS

For a special treat put a chocolate wrapped candy under your house guests pillow. A European custom.

⅓ c. dried apricots   ¼ c. walnuts
1 c. pitted prunes   ⅓ c. sugar
¼ c. raisins

Pour boiling water over apricots to cover; let stand till cool. Drain well. Grind fruits and nuts through coarse blade of food grinder. Stir in sugar. Form into ½ inch balls. Dip in melted chocolate or almond bark. Makes 3½ to 4 dozen.

CHERRY CORDIALS

Dip chocolate on a clear, cool day. The temperature should be from 60° to 70° in the dipping room. Cool the chocolate free from steam, air conditioning, but no draft. These conditions affect the color and gloss of the chocolate.

1 (10 oz.) jar maraschino cherries   ⅓ recipe fondant (see Mint Fondant
   with stems   Patties)
Brandy or orange liqueur

Drain syrup from cherries. Add brandy or liqueur to jar to cover cherries. Cover; let stand 8 to 10 hours or overnight. Drain cherries well, reserving brandy or liqueur for another use. Let cherries stand on paper toweling till dry. Melt fondant in a small bowl or saucepan set in a large pan of hot water. Add water to fondant, a few drops at a time, just till dipping consistency (coats cherry easily). Dip cherries completely in melted fondant. Let dry on waxed paper. Dip completely in melted chocolate or almond bark as directed for dip-your-own candies. Let stand in a cool, dry place for 4 or 5 days to ripen (fondant begins to liquefy). Makes about 2 dozen.

MINT FONDANT PATTIES

Use two-thirds of the fondant for patties, and the remaining third for Cherry Cordials.

Butter   ¼ tsp. cream of tartar
3 c. granulated sugar   10 drops of peppermint extract
1 c. boiling water

To make fondant, butter sides of heavy 1½ quart saucepan. In prepared pan, combine sugar, water, and cream of tartar. Stir over medium heat till sugar dissolves and mixture boils. Cover; cook 30 to 45 seconds. Uncover and boil, without stirring, to soft ball stage (240°). Immediately pour onto platter. Do not scrape pan. Cool till candy feels only slightly warm to touch, about 40 minutes; do not stir candy. Using spatula or wooden spoon, scrape candy from edge of platter toward center, then work till creamy and stiff, 5 to 6 minutes. Knead with fingers till smooth and free from lumps, 2 minutes. Wrap in plastic wrap; place in covered container to ripen 24 hours. Reserve a third of the fondant for Cherry Cordials. Knead remaining two-thirds of the fondant with peppermint extract. Shape into 1 inch patties; place on waxed paper. Let dry at room temperature for 2 to 3 hours. Dip in melted chocolate or almond bark. Makes 1 pound fondant.

CHOCOLATE FONDUE

Finely grate or chop the chocolate for easier melting.

6 oz. good quality bittersweet chocolate
6 oz. good quality milk chocolate

½ c. heavy cream
3 Tbsp. Grand Marnier

Chop chocolates coarsely; place in medium saucepan with cream and Grand Marnier. Cook, stirring constantly, over very low heat until chocolate is melted and mixture is thick and smooth. Transfer to fondue pot or saucepan; keep warm over very low heat. Serve with assortment of dunkable fruits and tidbits. Serves 6.

VALENTINE LOVE BITES

Chocolate place cards! A novel idea. One your guests will enjoy.

In small heavy saucepan over very low heat; melt one 8 ounce package semi-sweet chocolate and ¼ cup butter, stirring frequently until blended and smooth. Remove from heat; stir in 2 teaspoons grated orange peel and ½ teaspoon orange extract. Pour chocolate mixture into foil lined 8 inch square baking pan. Place in freezer 5 minutes until set. Remove pan from freezer; with sharp knife or scallop-edged pastry wheel, cut chocolate into eight 4x2 inch rectangles. Remove from pan; peel off foil. Decorate rectangles with messages and hearts, as desired, using red or white prepared decorating icing. Makes 8 greeting or place cards.

CAROB PEANUT CLUSTERS

Carob, a chocolate substitute, is used in this delicious candy.

1 c. quick cooking rolled oats
1 c. sugar
3 Tbsp. carob powder
⅓ c. evaporated milk

¼ c. butter
¼ c. peanut butter
½ c. peanuts

To toast oats, place oats in a layer in 15x10x1 inch baking pan. Bake in 350° oven for 15 to 20 minutes, stirring occasionally. In a saucepan, combine sugar and carob powder; add milk and butter. Bring to a full rolling boil over medium heat. Boil gently 1 minute, stirring constantly. Remove from heat. Stir in peanut butter. Pour over oats and peanuts in a bowl; stir to combine. Let cool slightly. Drop by teaspoons onto waxed paper. Chill. Makes 36 pieces.

CHOCO-NUT CANDY

In melting chocolate it is very important that no water get into the chocolate.

1 (6 oz.) pkg. semi-sweet chocolate morsels
3 Tbsp. honey

⅛ tsp. salt
1 tsp. vanilla
1 c. coarsely chopped pecans

Combine chocolate morsels and honey in top of double boiler; bring water to a boil. Reduce heat to low and cook until chocolate melts. Stir in remaining ingredients; spread into a buttered 8 inch square pan. Chill. Cut into squares. Store in refrigerator. Makes 25 squares.

CHOCOLATE LACE TRAY

Chocolate lover's dreams are answered with this amazing sweet, and it's so easy to make! Just drizzle the melted German's sweet chocolate over a chilled foil form; chill it again and then remove the chocolate from the foil.

2½ (4 oz.) bars German's sweet   1 recipe Dipped fruit
  cooking chocolate (10 oz.)
1 recipe Petite Spice Cakes (see
  index for recipe)

1. Press a large piece of heavy-duty foil on the bottom and up the sides of a shallow 1 quart au gratin dish. Chill in freezer.

2. In a heavy 1½ quart saucepan, melt the German's chocolate over low heat, stirring till smooth. *Do not add any liquid.* Using a small spoon, drizzle about half of the melted chocolate randomly over the bottom and up the sides of the chilled foil inside the au gratin dish. (Or, pipe melted chocolate through a pastry bag fitted with a writing tip.) Return to the freezer about 5 minutes or till firm. (Reheat chocolate if it becomes too thick.) Repeat drizzling with remaining melted chocolate over the bottom and up the sides of the foil lined dish. Chill in the freezer for 15 minutes more.

3. To unmold chocolate tray, lift the chocolate coated foil from dish. Carefully peel foil from chocolate. Using wide metal spatulas, transfer chocolate tray to a serving platter; chill up to 24 hours. Serve topped with cakes and fruit. Makes 6 to 8 servings.

Dipped Fruit: In separate small saucepans melt 2 ounces white confectioners coating, 2 ounces milk chocolate, and 2 ounces German's sweet cooking chocolate. (Or, place in small nonmetal bowls and melt in your microwave oven.) Using your choice of glaceed or non-juicy fresh fruits, place one piece of fruit on end of a wooden skewer. Dip a portion of the fruit into each melted mixture, forming layers by dipping deeply into one, less deeply into the next, and just the tip into the last. Place on a waxed paper lined pan; chill till firm or up to 2 hours.

CAROB CANDY SQUARES

You can find roasted soybeans in health food stores. Roasting gives soybeans the flavor of roasted peanuts.

½ c. honey   1 c. roasted soybeans or dry
½ c. creamy peanut butter   roasted peanuts
½ c. unsweetened carob powder or   1 c. raisins, cut up pitted dates, or
  1 (1 oz.) sq. unsweetened   cut up pitted figs
  chocolate, melted   1 c. flaked coconut

In a medium saucepan, stir together honey and peanut butter over low heat just till melted. Remove from heat; stir in carob or chocolate till well blended. Stir in soybeans, raisins, and ¾ cup of the coconut till well coated. Press mixture into a waxed paper lined 9x5x3 inch loaf pan. Sprinkle surface with remaining coconut; press lightly into candy. Cover and chill till firm. Cut into squares to serve. Store, covered, in refrigerator. Makes 24 pieces.

NUTTY COCONUT CANDY BARS

Combine cherries, chocolate, and coconut to make this heavenly candy.

3¼ c. sifted confectioners sugar
1 (3 oz.) pkg. cream cheese
1 tsp. vanilla
1⅓ c. coconut

½ c. chopped candied cherries
1 lb. chocolate flavored
   confectioners coating

Butter baking sheet; set aside. Combine sugar, cheese, and vanilla till crumbly. Stir in coconut and cherries. Knead till blended. Turn out onto foil. Pat into a 10x5 inch rectangle. Chill 30 minutes. Cut into 2x1 inch rectangles. Dip, one at a time, into melted coating. Dry on waxed paper. Makes 25.

CRUNCHY CHEWY CHOCOLATE BARS

An especially delicious chocolate candy.

½ c. granulated sugar
¼ c. butter
¼ c. light cream or milk
1 c. tiny marshmallows
2 c. sifted confectioners sugar
¾ c. chopped peanuts

1½ c. vanilla caramels
2 Tbsp. butter
1 Tbsp. light cream or milk
1 lb. chocolate flavored
   confectioners coating

Line an 8x8x2 inch baking pan with foil; extend over edges. Butter foil. In saucepan, combine sugar, the ¼ cup butter, and the ¼ cup cream. Cook over medium heat to boiling 6 to 8 minutes, stirring constantly. Cook over heat 3 minutes more; stir occasionally. Mixture should boil at a moderate, steady rate over entire surface. Remove from heat. Add marshmallows; stir till melted. Stir in confectioners sugar, then chopped peanuts. Spread evenly in pan. Cool 20 minutes.

In a heavy 1½ quart saucepan, combine caramels, the remaining butter, and cream. Cook over low heat till caramels are melted; stir occasionally. Pour over mixture in pan. Chill 1 hour. When firm, use foil to lift out of pan; invert. Cut into 2x1 inch rectangles.

Melt confectioners coating. Dip rectangles, one at a time, into coating. Sprinkle additional peanuts on top. Dry on waxed paper. Store, tightly covered, in a cool dry place. Makes 32.

CHOCOLATE-PEPPERMINT FONDUE

So fancy and delicious. Perfect for a buffet dinner party.

Melt 1 (6 oz.) package semi-sweet chocolate pieces with 1 tablespoon shortening on HIGH for 2½ to 3 minutes; stir until smooth. Add 1 (5 ounce) can evaporated milk and 1 (1.5 ounce) chocolate covered peppermint candy; heat on MEDIUM (50% powder) for 2½ to 3 minutes, then stir. Serve with luscious strawberries or as a sauce on ice cream.

CHEESECAKES

HEAVENLY CHOCOLATE CHEESECAKE

Is there anything better than chocolate cheesecake?

2 c. vanilla wafers, finely crushed
1 c. ground toasted almonds
½ c. butter, melted
½ c. sugar
1 (12 oz.) pkg. (2 c.) milk chocolate
   morsels
½ c. milk

1 env. unflavored gelatin
2 (8 oz.) pkg. cream cheese,
   softened
½ c. sour cream
½ tsp. almond flavoring
½ c. heavy cream, whipped

In bowl combine vanilla wafer crumbs, almonds, butter, and sugar; mix well. Pat firmly into 9 inch springform pan, covering bottom and 2 inches up sides; set aside. Melt over hot (not boiling) water, milk chocolate morsels; stir until smooth. Set aside. Pour milk in saucepan; sprinkle gelatin on top. Set aside for 1 minute. Cook over low heat, stirring constantly until gelatin dissolves. Set aside. In bowl, combine cream cheese, sour cream, and melted morsels; beat until fluffy. Beat in gelatin mixture and almond flavoring. Fold in whipped cream. Pour into prepared pan. Chill; remove rim. Makes one 9 inch cheesecake.

CHOCOLATE SWIRL CHEESECAKE

Definitely a prize winner!

2 c. graham cracker crumbs
1½ tsp. ground cinnamon
½ c. butter, melted
2 (1 oz.) sq. semi-sweet chocolate
2 (8 oz.) pkg. cream cheese,
   softened
1 c. sugar

6 eggs
¼ c. plus 1 Tbsp. all-purpose flour
1½ tsp. grated lemon rind
3 Tbsp. lemon juice
1 tsp. vanilla
1 c. whipping cream, whipped
Grated chocolate (optional)

Combine graham cracker crumbs, cinnamon, and butter, mixing well; firmly press into bottom and up sides of a 9 inch springform pan, then refrigerate.

Place chocolate in top of a double boiler; bring water to a boil. Reduce heat to low; cook until chocolate melts. Set aside to cool slightly.

Beat cream cheese with electric mixer until light and fluffy; gradually add sugar, mixing well. Add eggs, one at a time, beating after each addition; stir in flour, lemon rind, lemon juice, and vanilla. Fold whipped cream into the cream cheese mixture.

Combine 1 cup cheesecake mixture and melted chocolate; set aside. Pour remaining cheesecake mixture into prepared crust. Pour chocolate mixture over top of cheesecake mixture; gently swirl with a knife.

Bake at 300° for 1 hour. Turn off oven and let cheesecake stand in closed oven for 1 hour. Open oven door, and allow cheesecake to stand in oven 2 to 3 hours or until completely cooled. Chill several hours. Garnish with grated chocolate if desired. Makes one 9 inch cheesecake.

CHOCOLATE CHEESE CAKE

Absolutely none better!

Crumb Crust:

1 (8½ oz.) pkg. chocolate wafers, crushed fine (about 2 c.)
¼ c. granulated sugar

1 tsp. ground cinnamon
6 Tbsp. butter, melted

Filling:

3 (8 oz.) pkg. cream cheese (at room temperature)
1 c. granulated sugar
1 c. (6 oz.) semi-sweet chocolate chips, melted and cooled

3 Tbsp. all-purpose flour
3 large eggs (at room temperature)
2 Tbsp. heavy cream
2 tsp. vanilla

Topping:

¾ c. sour cream
¾ tsp. vanilla

¼ c. semi-sweet chocolate mini chips

Heat oven to 400°. Have a 9 inch springform pan ready.

Crust: Thoroughly mix crust ingredients in small bowl. Press firmly onto bottom and 2 inches up sides of ungreased springform pan. Bake for 10 minutes. Remove from oven to rack to cool. Reduce oven temperature to 300°.

Filling: Beat cream cheese in large bowl with electric mixer until smooth. Add sugar, chocolate, and flour; beat until well blended and fluffy. Add eggs, one at a time, beating well after each. Beat in cream and vanilla. Pour into cooled crust. Bake in middle of oven for 60 to 65 minutes until filling is set. Remove to rack to cool 10 minutes. Carefully run small spatula between sides of pan and crust to loosen. Do not remove sides.

Topping: Mix sour cream and vanilla in small bowl until smooth. Spread over cheese cake. Arrange mini chips in lattice pattern on top. Chill several hours or overnight before removing sides of pan. Makes 16 servings.

INDIVIDUAL CHEESECAKES

Individual cheesecakes in a chocolate crust.

14 chocolate wafer cookies
4 (3 oz.) pkg. cream cheese, softened
⅔ c. sugar
2 eggs
1 tsp. vanilla

¾ c. commercial sour cream
¼ c. sugar
1 (10 oz.) pkg. frozen sliced strawberries, thawed and drained

Line muffin pans with paper liners. Place a chocolate wafer in each cup. Set pans aside.

Beat cream cheese with electric mixer until light and fluffy; gradually add ⅔ cup sugar and mix well. Add eggs and vanilla, beating well. Spoon mixture into liners filling two-thirds full. Bake at 350° for 10 minutes. Cool.

Combine sour cream and ¼ cup sugar; mix well. Spread over each cheesecake. Top each with a heaping teaspoonful of strawberries. Freeze until firm. Remove from freezer 5 minutes before serving. Makes 14 servings.

TWO-TONE CHEESECAKE

This recipe makes a very large cheesecake.

1½ c. crushed chocolate wafers (about 30 cookies)
4 Tbsp. butter (½ stick), softened
5 (8 oz.) pkg. cream cheese, softened
1¾ c. sugar
5 eggs
¼ c. milk

3 Tbsp. all-purpose flour
2 sq. semi-sweet chocolate
1 tsp. grated lemon peel
1 tsp. instant espresso coffee powder
½ c. sour cream
Lemon leaves or other nontoxic leaves (for garnish)

Early in day or day ahead:

1. In 10 x 2½ inch springform pan, with hand, mix chocolate wafers and butter; press onto bottom and halfway up side of pan to form a scalloped edge. Set aside.

2. In large bowl, with mixer at medium speed, beat cream cheese just until smooth; slowly beat in sugar. With mixer at low speed, beat in eggs, milk, and flour just until blended, occasionally scraping bowl.

3. Preheat oven to 300°F. In heavy small saucepan over low heat, melt chocolate, stirring frequently. Pour 5½ cups cream cheese mixture into another large bowl; stir in lemon peel. Pour lemon cream cheese mixture into crust in pan.

4. Into remaining cream cheese mixture, with mixer at low speed, beat melted chocolate and espresso coffee powder until blended. Gently spoon chocolate cream cheese mixture on top of mixture in pan. Bake cheesecake 55 minutes. Turn off oven; let cheesecake remain in oven until cooked, about 2 hours. Refrigerate cheesecake at least 4 hours or until well chilled.

5. To serve, remove side of springform pan. Spoon sour cream in center on top of cake. Garnish with lemon leaves. Makes 20 servings.

HEAVENLY KAHLUA CHEESECAKE

A very sophisticated chocolate cheesecake.

1¼ c. graham cracker crumbs
¼ c. sugar
¼ c. cocoa
⅓ c. butter, melted
2 (8 oz.) pkg. cream cheese, softened
¾ c. sugar
½ c. cocoa
2 eggs

¼ c. strong coffee
¼ c. Kahlua or other coffee flavored liqueur
1 tsp. vanilla
1 c. commercial sour cream
2 Tbsp. sugar
1 tsp. vanilla
6 to 8 chocolate curls (optional)

Combine first 4 ingredients; mix well. Firmly press mixture into bottom of a 9 inch springform pan. Bake at 325° for 5 minutes; cool.

Beat cream cheese with electric mixer until light and fluffy; gradually add ¾ cup sugar, mixing well. Beat in ½ cup cocoa. Add eggs, one at a time, beating well after each addition. Stir in next 3 ingredients. Pour into prepared pan. Bake at 375° for 25 minutes. (Filling will be soft but will firm up as cake stands.)

Combine sour cream, 2 tablespoons sugar, and 1 teaspoon vanilla; spread over hot cheesecake. Bake at 425° for 5 to 7 minutes. Let cool to room temperature on a wire rack; chill 8 hours or overnight.

Remove sides of springform pan. To garnish, place 3 chocolate curls in center of cheesecake; gently break remaining chocolate curls and sprinkle over cheesecake if desired. Makes 10 to 12 servings.

RASPBERRY CHEESECAKE WITH CHOCOLATE WAFERS

One of the best cheesecakes. The bottoms of the wafers become wonderfully chewy while the tops stay crisp.

2½ c. cottage cheese
2 c. sour cream (1 pt.)
4 oz. cream cheese (at room temperature)
½ c. confectioners sugar
1 tsp. vanilla
1 c. red raspberry preserves (12 oz. jar)

2 env. unflavored gelatin
2 Tbsp. cold water
24 round chocolate wafers (an 8½ oz. pkg. has 36)
6 round chocolate wafers, crushed fine (about ⅓ c.)
Fresh raspberries (for garnish)

In food processor, process cottage cheese, sour cream, cream cheese, sugar, and vanilla until smooth. Transfer to a large bowl. (Or beat in large bowl with an electric mixer until smooth.) Mix preserves, gelatin, and water in a small saucepan. Let stand 1 minute. Bring to a simmer over low heat. Cook, stirring constantly, until preserves have melted and gelatin is completely dissolved. Cool slightly; fold into cheese mixture until blended. Chill, stirring every 30 minutes, about 1½ hours or until mixture mounds when dropped from a spoon. Pour into lightly oiled 9 inch springform pan. Stick chocolate wafers halfway into top of cake like spokes of a wheel. Chill 4 hours or overnight. Remove sides of pan; press wafer crumbs against sides of cake in decorative pattern. Place raspberries between wafers on top. Makes 12 servings.

Notes

FANCY FROZEN DESSERTS, ICE CREAMS, AND THEIR SAUCES

ORANGE-CHOCOLATE SAUCE

Make this special sauce with white and milk chocolate!

In heavy 1 quart saucepan over very low heat, melt one 3 ounce package white chocolate and one 1 ounce square milk chocolate, stirring frequently until smooth. Gradually stir in ¾ cup heavy cream or milk; cook, stirring frequently until mixture is smooth and heated through. Makes about 1¼ cups.

CHOCOLATE SANDWICH-COOKIE CAKE

An extra special chocolate dessert. This 3 ingredient cake uses one of the most popular cookies around and can be made up to 3 days ahead and frozen. It's a natural party cake.

2 c. whipping cream
¼ c. almond flavored liqueur
1 (16 oz.) pkg. chocolate sandwich cookies (about 42)

Sliced strawberries and/or chocolate sandwich cookies (optional for garnish)

Mix whipping cream and liqueur in large bowl; chill 30 minutes. Coarsely chop cookies; place in medium size bowl. Beat cream mixture with electric mixer until firm peaks form when beaters are lifted. Add ½ cup to chopped cookies; mix well with rubber spatula. Spoon one-third of the cookie mixture onto bottom of lightly greased 7 to 8 inch springform pan. Pat to spread evenly over bottom. Spoon one-third of the remaining whipped cream on top; spread evenly to edges. Spoon half the remaining cookie mixture evenly over the cream. Repeat layers with remaining cream and cookie mixture, ending with cream. Freeze at least 2 hours, or wrap airtight and freeze up to 3 days. About 1 hour before serving, run long thin knife around edges of cake to loosen; remove sides of pan. Place cake in refrigerator to thaw slightly (cake is served semi-frozen). Just before serving garnish with strawberries and cookies. Serves 8.

ARCTIC MOUSSE

A frozen mousse with a rich, chocolate taste.

1¼ c. graham cracker crumbs
¼ c. sugar
⅓ c. butter, melted
1 (7 oz.) jar marshmallow creme
2 (1 oz.) sq. unsweetened chocolate, melted

1 tsp. vanilla
2 Tbsp. milk
1 c. whipping cream, whipped

Combine crumbs, sugar, and butter. Press onto bottom of 8 inch square pan. Combine marshmallow creme, chocolate, and vanilla; mix until well blended. Gradually add milk, blending until smooth. Fold in whipped cream. Pour into pan; freeze. Sprinkle with additional crumbs or garnish with chocolate curls, if desired. Serves 6 to 8.

DOUBLE CHOCOLATE CHUNK ICE CREAM

This ice cream is absolutely heaven!

2 c. sugar
2 env. unflavored gelatin
4 c. light cream
4 sq. (4 oz.) unsweetened
    chocolate, chopped

2 beaten eggs
4 c. whipping cream
1 c. finely chopped milk chocolate
    (about 6 oz.)

In a saucepan, combine sugar and gelatin. Stir in light cream and unsweetened chocolate. Cook and stir over medium heat till mixture almost boils, sugar dissolves, and chocolate melts. Stir 1 cup of hot mixture into eggs; return all to saucepan. Cook and stir 2 minutes more. (If chocolate flecks appear, beat till smooth.) Cover; chill.

Stir in whipping cream and milk chocolate. Freeze in a 4 or 5 quart ice cream freezer according to manufacturers directions. Makes about 2½ quarts.

CHOCOLATE-RAISIN ICE CREAM CAKE

A great combination: Rum-raisin ice cream and chocolate meringue.

Cocoa Meringue:

¾ c. plus 3 Tbsp. confectioners
    sugar
5 Tbsp. unsweetened cocoa powder

5 egg whites (room temperature)
¼ tsp. cream of tartar
10 Tbsp. sugar

Other ingredients:

3 pt. rum-raisin ice cream
½ c. whipping cream, well chilled

1 tsp. sugar

For meringue: Position 1 rack in center of oven and another in lower third; preheat to 180°F. (or lowest setting). Grease corners of 2 baking sheets and line with foil or parchment. Butter foil or paper and dust with flour. Using 9 inch springform pan as guide, trace circle on each sheet. Fit pastry bag with ½ inch plain tip. Sift confectioners sugar with cocoa. Beat whites with cream of tartar with electric mixer at medium speed until soft peaks form. Add 10 tablespoons sugar, 1 tablespoon at a time and beat until meringue is shiny. Gently fold in cocoa mixture.

Spoon meringue into prepared pastry bag. Pipe out meringue ¾ inch thick onto 1 circle on baking sheet, beginning at center and spiraling outward until circle is completely covered. Repeat with second circle. Replace pastry bag tip with medium star tip. Pipe remaining meringue onto empty portions of baking sheets into mounds ½ inch in diameter and 1 inch high with pointed tops, forming "kisses." Bake until kisses are firm and dry, about 1 to 1½ hours (depending on temperature of oven). To test, remove 1 kiss and cool 2 minutes. Break apart; it should be dry, crumbly, and not sticky.

Transfer kisses to rack. Continue baking layers until firm and dry, about 1½ hours. Gently release from paper, using large metal spatula. If bottom of meringue is sticky, return to pan and bake until dry. Remove from paper and cool on rack. (Can be prepared 1 week ahead. Store in airtight container.)

Soften ice cream in refrigerator until spreadable. Carefully trim meringue layers to fit 9 inch springform pan. Set 1 layer in pan. Spread with half of ice cream. Set second layer on top. Spread with remaining ice cream. Freeze at least 8 hours or overnight.

Just before serving, whip cream with 1 teaspoon sugar until soft peaks form. Set cake on platter. Run knife around edge of pan; release sides. Smooth whipped cream in thin layer over top and sides of cake, using metal spatula. Decorate top with meringue kisses. Serves 10 to 12.

CHOCOLATE MOUSSE ICE CREAM

Absolutely one of the best ice creams!

¾ c. sugar
¾ c. water
1 lb. semi-sweet chocolate,
    chopped

6 egg yolks
1 qt. whipping cream, whipped to
    soft peaks
Fresh fruit

Heat sugar and water in heavy medium saucepan over low heat, swirling pan occasionally, until sugar dissolves. Increase heat to medium and boil 3 minutes, swirling pan occasionally. Remove from heat and gradually add chocolate, stirring until smooth. Cool.

Beat yolks to blend. Mix in chocolate. Cool to room temperature, stirring occasionally, about 1 hour.

Fold 1 cup cream into chocolate mixture, then fold in remaining cream. Transfer mixture to ice cream maker and process according to manufacturer's instructions. Freeze in covered container until firm, 1 to 2 hours.

Line baking sheet with waxed paper. Scoop ice cream into balls and place on prepared sheet. Freeze until firm.

Just before serving, mound ice cream in glass bowl or on platter and then surround with fresh fruit. Makes about 2 quarts.

FUDGY CHOCOLATE NUT ICE CREAM

Just delicious on a summer day.

5 (1 oz.) sq. unsweetened
    chocolate, melted and cooled
1 (14 oz.) can sweetened
    condensed milk (not
    evaporated milk)
4 egg yolks*

2 tsp. vanilla
2 c. (1 pt.) half & half
2 c. (1 pt.) whipping cream
    (unwhipped)
1 c. chopped nuts

In large mixer bowl, beat chocolate, condensed milk, egg yolks, and vanilla; mix well. Stir in half & half, then whipping cream and nuts. Pour into ice cream container. Freeze according to manufacturer's instructions. Store leftovers in freezer. Makes about 1½ quarts.

Refrigerator-Freezer method: Omit half & half. Reduce chocolate to 3 (1 ounce) squares. Whip whipping cream. Combine chocolate, condensed milk, egg yolks, and vanilla as the preceding. Fold in whipped cream and nuts. Pour into 9x5 inch loaf pan or other 2 quart container; cover. Freeze 6 hours or until firm. Return leftovers to freezer.

* Use only Grade A clean, uncracked eggs.

CHERRY CHOCOLATE SUNDAES

Made with chocolate wafers. A good way to empty the cookie jar!

½ c. cherry pie filling
¼ tsp. ground cinnamon
¼ tsp. grated lemon peel

Chocolate wafer cookies
½ pt. vanilla ice cream, softened

1. In small bowl, mix cherry pie filling, cinnamon, and lemon peel. Coarsely chop enough cookies to measure ⅓ cup.

2. To serve, spoon vanilla ice cream into 2 dessert bowls. Spoon cherry pie filling mixture over ice cream; sprinkle sundaes with chopped cookies. Makes 2 servings.

QUEEN OF SHEBA ICE CREAM CAKE

This dark chocolate cake is a wonderful do-ahead party dessert. Perfect for ladies bridge club.

Cocoa-Almond Cake:

½ c. blanched almonds, toasted
8 Tbsp. sugar
¼ c. all-purpose flour
2 Tbsp. unsweetened cocoa powder
½ tsp. baking powder

3 eggs, separated (room
    temperature)
Pinch of cream of tartar
¼ c. (½ stick) unsalted butter,
    melted and cooled

Chocolate Parfait:

6 oz. semi-sweet chocolate,
    coarsely chopped
½ c. milk
4 egg yolks (room temperature)

⅔ c. sugar
1 c. whipping cream, well chilled
¼ c. Amaretto liqueur
2 Tbsp. water

Chocolate Whipped Cream:

1 oz. semi-sweet chocolate,
    coarsely chopped
½ c. whipping cream, well chilled

2 tsp. sugar
½ tsp. vanilla
7 whole blanched almonds

For cake: Position rack in center of oven and preheat to 350°F. Cover base of 9 inch springform pan with foil, then attach sides. Butter and flour foil and pan sides. Finely grind almonds with 2 tablespoons sugar in processor. Sift flour, cocoa, and baking powder into small bowl. Stir in almond mixture. Beat yolks and 4 tablespoons sugar using electric mixer until slowly dissolving ribbon forms when beaters are lifted, about 5 minutes. Beat whites with cream of tartar in another bowl until stiff but not dry. Gradually add remaining 2 tablespoon sugar and beat until whites are stiff and shiny. Fold ⅓ of almond-cocoa mixture into yolks, then ⅓ of whites. Repeat twice, folding in butter just before final ⅓ of whites is incorporated. Spoon batter into prepared pan, smoothing surface with spatula. Bake until tester inserted into center of cake comes out dry, about 20 minutes. Cool in pan on rack 5 minutes. Invert onto rack and cool completely.

For parfait: Melt chocolate in top of double boiler over hot, but not boiling, water. Bring milk to simmer in heavy medium saucepan over low heat. Whisk yolks and sugar in bowl until smooth. Gradually whisk in hot milk; return to saucepan. Stir over low heat until mixture leaves path on back of spoon when finger is drawn across, about 5 minutes; *do not boil*. Gradually whisk custard into chocolate until smooth. Cool completely, stirring occasionally.

Whip cream to soft peaks. Fold in chocolate mixture in 3 batches.

To assemble: Cut cake into 2 layers, using serrated knife. Set bottom layer, cut side up, in 9 inch springform pan. Combine liqueur and 2 tablespoons water. Brush 3 tablespoons onto cake in pan. Spoon half of Chocolate Parfait over, spreading to edge of cake. Top with second layer, cut side up. Brush with remaining liqueur. Spread with remaining parfait. Cover and freeze until firm, at least 4 hours.

Remove pan sides. Refrigerate cake while preparing cream.

For whipped cream: Melt chocolate in double boiler over hot, but not boiling, water. Stir until smooth. Remove from over water. Whip cream with sugar and vanilla to stiff peaks. Whisk in chocolate. Spoon mixture into pastry bag fitted with medium star tip. Set cake on platter. Pipe 12 rosettes of chocolate cream around top edges of cake and 1 large rosette in center. Set almond on alternate rosettes and in center. Serve immediately. Serves 10 to 12.

CHOCOLATE-COFFEE FROZEN DESSERT

An especially fine flavored chocolate dessert.

2 c. vanilla wafer crumbs, divided	2 c. sifted confectioners sugar
¼ c. butter	1 tsp. vanilla
2½ (1 oz.) sq. unsweetened chocolate	3 eggs, separated
	1 c. coarsely chopped pecans
½ c. butter	2 qt. coffee ice cream, softened

Combine 1¾ cups vanilla wafer crumbs and ¼ cup melted butter, mixing well. Press into a 13x9x2 inch pan. Set aside.

Combine chocolate and ½ cup butter in a heavy saucepan; cook over low heat until melted. Remove from heat. Add confectioners sugar and vanilla; beat 2 minutes at medium speed of electric mixer. Add egg yolks, beating until smooth.

Beat egg whites (at room temperature) until stiff peaks form; fold into chocolate mixture. Spread mixture over crumbs and sprinkle with pecans. Cover and freeze until firm.

Spread ice cream over pecan layer; sprinkle with remaining ¼ cup crumbs. Cover and freeze overnight or until ice cream is firm. Makes 15 to 18 servings.

CHOCOLATE-CHIP COFFEE ICE CREAM CAKE

There will be leftover cookies to serve with this elegant cake.

Chocolate Chip Cookies:

1 c. all-purpose flour
½ tsp. salt
½ tsp. baking soda
½ c. (1 stick) unsalted butter (room temperature)
½ c. firmly packed light brown sugar

¼ c. sugar
1 egg
½ tsp. vanilla
1 c. walnuts, coarsely chopped
¾ c. semi-sweet chocolate chips

Other ingredients:

½ c. coffee bean candies*
2 pt. coffee ice cream
1 c. whipping cream, well chilled

1 Tbsp. sugar
1 tsp. coffee extract or 2 Tbsp. coffee liqueur

For cookies: Preheat oven to 350°F. Butter baking sheets. Sift flour, salt, and baking soda. Cream butter using electric mixer. Beat in sugars until smooth. Beat in egg and vanilla. Stir in flour mixture, then nuts and chocolate chips. Drop dough onto prepared sheets, using 1½ teaspoons for each cookie and spacing 2 inches apart. Flatten with back of fork dipped in water. Bake until cookies are lightly browned, about 7 minutes. Cool completely on racks. (Cookies can be prepared 1 week ahead. Store in airtight containers.)

* Reserve 21 coffee beans; coarsely chop remainder. Soften ice cream in refrigerator until spreadable.

Oil 8x4 inch loaf pan lined with aluminum foil. Cover pan bottom with a layer of cookies, flat sides down, fitting together tightly. Cover with half of ice cream, pressing firmly with back of spoon. Sprinkle with chopped coffee beans. Crumble 4 cookies and sprinkle over top. Add remaining ice cream, pressing firmly. Smooth top with spatula. Top with layer of 8 cookies, flat sides up, fitting together tightly. Cover and freeze at least 1 day.

Just before serving, run knife around edge of dessert. Invert onto platter. Refrigerate while prepared cream. Whip cream with 1 tablespoon sugar and coffee extract until stiff peaks form. Smooth ¾ of cream over sides of cake. Spoon remainder into pastry bag fitted with medium star tip. Pipe rosettes over top of cake. Decorate top with reserved coffee beans. Freeze 5 minutes. Serve. Serves 8 to 10.

CHOCOLATE-NUT SHERBET

This sherbet is so easy you don't need an ice cream freezer.

2 eggs
⅔ c. sugar
2 c. milk

¼ c. light corn syrup
¼ c. chocolate flavored syrup
½ c. chopped walnuts

In small mixer bowl, beat eggs at high speed on electric mixer till thick and lemon colored, about 4 minutes. Gradually add sugar, beating till thick. Stir in milk, corn syrup, and chocolate syrup. Pour mixture into two 3 cup freezer trays or one

8x8x2 inch pan; freeze firm, about 2½ hours. Break sherbet in chunks into chilled mixer bowl; beat till smooth. Stir in walnuts. Immediately return mixture to cold trays or pan. Freeze firm, several hours or overnight. Makes about 5 cups.

CHOCOLATE-CREME DE MENTHE PARFAITS

This chocolate dessert is just pure elegance.

3 Tbsp. chocolate syrup
3 Tbsp. creme de menthe
1 qt. vanilla ice cream

Whipped cream
Mint leaves (optional)

Combine chocolate syrup and creme de menthe in a small bowl; mix well. Spoon 1½ teaspoons chocolate mixture into each of six (6 ounce) chilled parfait glasses; spoon in ⅓ cup ice cream. Repeat layers. Cover and freeze until firm. Remove parfaits several minutes before serving; top with a dollop of whipped cream. Garnish them with mint leaves, if desired. Makes 6 servings.

SUPER-EASY ORANGE CHOCOLATE CHIP ICE CREAM MOLD

Combine chocolate and orange juice for this very rich, almost sinful dessert.

2 c. heavy cream
½ c. granulated sugar
½ c. thawed frozen orange juice
  concentrate

½ c. semi-sweet chocolate mini
  chips
Orange slices, cut in quarters (for
  garnish)

Place a 3 cup mold in refrigerator to chill. Stir cream, sugar, and orange juice in a medium size bowl until sugar dissolves. Place in freezer 1½ hours or until partially frozen (mixture must be thick so chips won't sink). Fold in chocolate chips. Pour into chilled mold; cover and freeze until hard, several hours or overnight. To unmold, run tip of sharp knife around rim. Place upside down on serving platter but don't remove mold. Refrigerate 30 minutes or until mold can be lifted and removed. Garnish with border of orange slices, then return to freezer until serving time. Makes 6 servings.

GIANT ICE CREAM COOKIE SANDWICH

A fun to eat chocolate dessert.

¾ c. all-purpose flour
¾ tsp. baking soda
½ c. butter (at room temperature)
⅓ c. packed brown sugar
1 tsp. vanilla
1¼ c. old-fashioned oats

⅓ c. plus 2 Tbsp. semi-sweet
  chocolate chips
1 qt. vanilla ice cream, slightly
  softened
⅓ c. semi-sweet chocolate mint
  chips (for garnish)

Heat oven to 350°. Lightly grease 2 cookie sheets. Mix flour and baking soda. In a large bowl, beat butter, sugar, and vanilla with electric mixer until fluffy. Stir in oats, flour mixture, and ⅓ cup chocolate chips until blended. Divide dough in half. Place half in middle of each cookie sheet and spread into an 8 inch circle. Sprinkle one with remaining 2 tablespoons chocolate chips, then score into 8 wedges with a sharp knife. Bake both 15 minutes, turning cookie sheets and switching oven positions once, until light browned and crisp-looking. Cool on sheets 10 minutes before removing to racks to cool completely. To assemble, cut scored cookie into 8 wedges. Place plain cookie flat side up on serving plate; quickly spread ice cream as evenly as possible over it. Arrange 7 cookie wedges on top (the eighth is for the cook). Press mini chips into ice cream around sides. Freeze until ice cream is firm. Cut between wedges to serve. Makes 7 servings.

CHOCOLATE ICE CREAM LINZER TORTE

Chocolate ice cream is sandwiched between layers of chocolate meringue, then covered with whipped cream and toasted almonds.

½ c. egg whites (about 5 eggs)
½ c. granulated sugar
1 c. sifted confectioners sugar
1 Tbsp. cornstarch
¼ c. unsweetened cocoa powder
½ c. toasted ground almonds
1 (12 oz.) jar raspberry preserves

1 qt. chocolate ice cream, softened
2 c. (1 pt.) heavy cream
⅔ c. toasted ground almonds
1 (12 oz.) pkg. frozen dry pack
  whole raspberries or 3 c. fresh
  raspberries

Preheat oven to slow (300°). Cut three 9 inch circles from plain brown paper. Place circles on cookie sheets. Beat egg whites in large bowl with electric mixer until soft peaks form. Slowly beat in the granulated sugar, 1 tablespoon at a time, until meringue forms stiff shiny peaks.

Sift together confectioners sugar, cornstarch, and cocoa onto wax paper. Gradually beat into meringue, 1 tablespoon at a time, beating just until blended. Fold in the ½ cup toasted almonds.

Spread meringue evenly over brown paper circles on the cookie sheets; spread to edge of circles. Bake in preheated slow oven (300°) for 45 minutes. Turn off oven; let meringue cool completely in oven with oven door closed.

Carefully remove cooled meringues from brown paper, being careful not to break or crack them. To assemble: Place 1 meringue layer on plate. Carefully spread one-third of the raspberry preserves over meringue. Spread with half the ice cream, smoothing the sides. Repeat with the second meringue layer and the other half of the ice cream. Top with remaining meringue layer. Press down gently to secure layers. Freeze until firm, about 3 hours.

To decorate: Beat heavy cream in medium size bowl until stiff. Frost top and sides of torte with about two-thirds of the whipped cream. Press the ⅔ cup toasted ground almonds into sides of torte. Spoon remaining whipped cream into pastry bag fitted with star tip; pipe rosettes around outer top edge of torte. Arrange raspberries in center. Top berries with remaining preserves. Serves 12.

Note: Meringue layers can be made several days ahead and stored in a tin with a tight fitting cover at room temperature.

FROZEN RASPBERRY CHOCOLATE CAKE

A fancy and delicious company dessert.

2 pt. (4 c.) whipping cream
7 oz. hard raspberry flavor candies, crushed fine (1¼ c.)
50 chocolate wafers (an 8½ oz. pkg. has 36)
2½ c. (14 oz.) coarsely chopped hard raspberry flavor candies (for garnish)

Softly whipped cream (for garnish)
6 round chocolate wafers, halved (for garnish)

Put an 8 inch springform pan in the freezer for 15 minutes to chill. Measure out and refrigerate ¼ cup cream for garnish. In a large bowl whip remaining cream with electric mixer until soft peaks form when beaters are lifted. Fold in crushed candy until blended. Remove pan from freezer. Pour cream mixture into chilled pan. Starting ½ inch in from sides of pan, stand wafers, rounded sides out, in a circle, pressing gently so they touch bottom of pan. Repeat in concentric circles, ½ inch apart, to center of pan. For center circle, break wafers in half and stand them up. Smooth top of filling. Freeze until firm, at least 4 hours or overnight. Just before serving, run a long thin knife dipped in hot water around edge of pan; remove sides of pan. Repeat with long bladed spatula across bottom to loosen. Remove to serving plate with 2 wide spatulas. Press additional chopped candies against sides of cake. Mound whipped cream in center of cake. Arrange wafer halves in cream. Keep frozen until ready to serve. Makes 12 servings.

RASPBERRY-BROWNIE ICE CREAM CAKE

This ice cream cake tops them all!

Fudge Brownies:

2 oz. semi-sweet chocolate, chopped
3 Tbsp. unsalted butter
4 Tbsp. plus 2 tsp. all-purpose flour
¼ tsp. baking powder
Pinch of salt

1 egg (room temperature)
½ c. sugar
½ tsp. vanilla
⅓ c. walnuts, coarsely chopped
1 pt. raspberry sherbet
2½ c. vanilla ice cream

Topping:

1 c. whipping cream, well chilled
2 tsp. sugar

1 tsp. vanilla
Fresh raspberries

For brownies: Position rack in center of oven and preheat to 350°F. Line 8 inch square pan with parchment or foil; butter paper or foil. Melt chocolate and 3 tablespoons butter in double boiler over hot, but not boiling, water. Stir until smooth. Cool slightly. Sift flour, baking powder, and salt. Blend egg and sugar using electric mixer. Mix in vanilla. Gradually beat in chocolate mixture. Stir in dry ingredients, then walnuts, using wooden spoon. Spread batter evenly in prepared pan. Bake until tester inserted in center comes out dry, about 19 minutes. Cool completely in pan on rack. Invert onto rack and remove paper. Cut into 16 squares; freeze brownies until firm but not solid, about 2 hours.

Line bottom of 8 inch square pan with waxed paper. Freeze about 15 minutes. Soften sherbet in refrigerator until spreadable. Smooth into prepared pan. Freeze until firm, about 15 minutes. Soften 1 cup ice cream in refrigerator until spreadable. Smooth over sherbet. Freeze until firm.

Cut each of the brownies into 2 layers. Cover ice cream with half of brownies, arranging around sides first, then filling in center. Press into ice cream. Freeze until firm, about 15 minutes.

Soften remaining 1½ cups ice cream in refrigerator. Spread over brownies. Freeze 15 minutes. Cover ice cream with remaining brownies, smooth sides up, arranging around sides first, then filling in center. Press into ice cream to even top. Cover and freeze for 8 hours or overnight.

Run knife around edges of dessert and invert onto platter; peel off parchment paper. Return to freezer.

For topping: Whip cream with sugar and vanilla until peaks form. Spoon into pastry bag fitted with medium star tip. Pipe mixture in ruffles over sides of cake. Pipe rosettes decoratively on top. Place raspberry atop each rosette. Serve with additional berries. Serves 8 to 10.

MINT CHOCOLATE CHIP AND FUDGE PIE

This refreshing and festive dessert involves no cooking at all.

1 (12 oz.) jar chocolate fudge
   topping
2 pt. chocolate chip ice cream
2 pt. mint chocolate chip ice cream

1 prepared 9 inch graham cracker
   crust
Fresh mint leaves (for garnish)

Soften fudge topping according to directions on the jar label. Scrape into a small bowl; stir to blend. Let stand about 5 minutes to cool slightly. Scoop 1 pint of each ice cream over bottom of crust, alternating flavors. Drizzle with half the fudge topping. Top with the remaining 2 pints of ice cream, building the scoops to a mound in the center. Drizzle with the remaining fudge topping. Freeze at least 5 hours or overnight. Transfer to refrigerator for 20 minutes before cutting into wedges and serving. Garnish with mint. Makes 10 servings.

COFFEE TARTUFFO PIE

A fine summertime pie! The flavors of chocolate and coffee together make this special pie.

3 pt. coffee ice cream
1 baked and cooled 9 inch
    chocolate-crumb crust (recipe
    follows)
12 maraschino or brandied
    cherries, stemmed (optional)
3 (1 oz.) sq. semi-sweet chocolate,
    melted

1 c. whipping cream
2 Tbsp. confectioners sugar
2 Tbsp. coffee flavor liqueur (such
    as Kahlua or Tia Maria,
    optional)

Scoop enough balls of ice cream into the crust to form a single layer on the bottom. Place 6 of the cherries at random on the ice cream. Top with the remaining ice cream, mounding balls slightly toward the center. Press down on ice cream with the back of the scoop, then smooth surface completely with a spatula. Freeze pie at least 5 hours or overnight. Grease a cookie sheet and line with wax paper. Pour melted chocolate onto waxed paper; spread evenly with metal spatula into a 10 inch square about ⅛ inch thick. Refrigerate 20 to 25 minutes until hard. Loosen from waxed paper and break into irregularly shaped pieces. Refrigerate in covered container until ready to use. Just before serving, whip cream in a chilled bowl until soft peaks form; fold in liqueur. Drop spoonfuls of cream around rim of pie (or use a pastry bag fitted with fluted tip). Decorate with remaining cherries; stand chocolate pieces randomly in pie. Serve at once or return to freezer until 10 minutes before serving. Makes 8 servings.

Chocolate-Crumb Crust:

24 chocolate wafers (an 8½ oz.
    pkg. has 36)

2 Tbsp. granulated sugar
3 Tbsp. butter, melted

Heat oven to 350°. Finely crush wafers in food processor or in plastic bag with rolling pin. Mix crumbs and sugar in a bowl. Drizzle with butter. Work with fork to coat thoroughly. Press crumbs in bottom and up sides of a 9 inch pie plate to form a crust. Bake for 10 minutes. Place pan on wire rack to cool completely before filling. Makes 1 (9 inch) crust.

CHOCOLATE-RASPBERRY CHOCOLATE CAKE

Two favorites teamed together make this delightful chocolate cake.

Chocolate-Cookie Layers:

½ c. butter (at room temperature)
1 c. packed light brown sugar
2 large eggs (at room temperature)
3 (1 oz.) sq. unsweetened
    chocolate, melted and cooled
1 tsp. vanilla
1 c. all-purpose flour

1 pt. raspberry sherbet
1 pt. chocolate ice cream
Chocolate curls (directions follow,
    for garnish)
Fresh raspberries (for garnish)
1 c. chocolate syrup (from can, jar,
    or bottle)

For cookie layers: Grease 2 cookie sheets (1 large 17x14 inch, 1 regular size 15x12 inch) lightly but evenly. Sprinkle them light with flour; tap off excess. Draw 2 circles on the large and 1 on the other cookie sheet with a wooden pick, using an 8 inch round layer cake pan as a guide. Heat oven to 350°. Beat butter and sugar in a medium size bowl with electric mixer until light and fluffy. Beat in eggs, one at a time, until well blended. Scrape sides and bottom of bowl occasionally. Stir in chocolate, then vanilla until well blended. Fold in flour until well blended. Spoon about ¾ cup batter in center of each circle on prepared cookie sheets. With a thin metal spatula, spread batter evenly just to edges of circles. Bake for 10 to 12 minutes, switching position of cookie sheets halfway through baking time for even cooking, until tops are firm to touch when lightly pressed. Cool on sheets on racks 5 minutes. With wide spatula carefully lift cookies to racks to cool completely.

To assemble: Put 1 cookie layer on a large sheet of foil. Scoop sherbet on top; smooth with back of a spoon. Top with second cookie layer and chocolate ice cream; smooth with back of spoon. Cover with remaining cookie layer. Wrap cake tightly in foil and freeze at least 5 hours or overnight. To serve, remove foil and place cake on serving platter. Garnish top with chocolate curls. Arrange berries to fill in spaces. Cut cake into wedges and serve on individual plates. Surround each wedge with a pool of chocolate syrup. Makes 10 servings.

Chocolate Curls: Unwrap 1 (1 ounce) square semi-sweet chocolate and put it on a piece of foil. Let stand in a warm place (90° to 100°), such as a cool oven or gas oven with burning pilot light, about 5 minutes or just until slightly softened. Chocolate should feel warm but still firm. (Or place paper wrapped chocolate in microwave on HIGH for about 30 seconds.) Using a vegetable peeler, shave chocolate from underside into curls with long, even strokes.

CLASSIC CHOCOLATE SAUCE

Definitely a special topper for ice cream.

2 (1 oz.) sq. unsweetened chocolate	½ tsp. salt
¼ c. butter	¾ c. evaporated milk
1¼ c. sugar	½ tsp. vanilla

Melt chocolate and butter in top of a double boiler; stir in remaining ingredients except vanilla. Cook over medium heat, stirring until sugar dissolves and sauce is smooth. Stir in vanilla. Serve warm over ice cream. Makes 2 cups.

COCOA-KAHLUA SUNDAES

Nothing could be better than Kahlua and chocolate!

2 Tbsp. plus 1 tsp. sugar	1 Tbsp. butter
2 Tbsp. plus 1 tsp. brown sugar	1 tsp. corn syrup
1 Tbsp. cocoa	1 pt. vanilla ice cream
2¼ tsp. all-purpose flour	¼ c. chopped pecans
¼ c. Kahlua or other coffee flavored liqueur	

Combine sugar, cocoa, and flour in a 2 cup glass measure. Stir in next 3 ingredients. Microwave at HIGH for 1½ to 2 minutes, or until thick and smooth, stirring after 1 minute.

Scoop ice cream into 2 individual serving dishes. Spoon sauce over ice cream and sprinkle with pecans. Serve immediately. Makes 2 servings.

CHOCOLATE ICE CREAM

A nice creamy and smooth textured chocolate ice cream.

**1 (12 oz.) can undiluted evaporated
 milk
4 sq. unsweetened chocolate
½ c. water**

**1 c. sugar
2 tsp. vanilla
2 Tbsp. butter**

Pour evaporated milk into small mixer bowl and freeze until ice crystals form around edge of bowl, about 45 minutes. Meanwhile, heat chocolate with water over low heat in saucepan. Stir until chocolate is melted and mixture is smooth. Add sugar; cook and stir until sugar is completely dissolved. Add vanilla. Measure ¾ cup into a small bowl; stir in butter and set aside for sauce. Chill remaining chocolate mixture.

Beat evaporated milk until soft peaks form. Fold in chilled chocolate mixture. Freeze in bowl until firm, 3 to 4 hours. Serve with the sauce. Garnish with coconut. Makes about 6 cups.

Ice Cream Sandwiches: For each sandwich, place one scoop of ice cream on a chocolate cookie. Let soften slightly, then cover with another cookie and press gently to form a sandwich. Serve immediately or store, wrapped in freezer.

MOCHA-MACAROON DESSERT

End a perfect dinner party with this fine chocolate dessert.

**1 pt. chocolate ice cream
1 c. crushed amaretti cookies
 (about 18 cookies)**

**3 Tbsp. coffee flavor liqueur
¼ c. heavy or whipping cream,
 whipped**

About 40 minutes before serving:

1. Let chocolate ice cream stand at room temperature 15 minutes to soften slightly.

2. Meanwhile, set aside 1 tablespoon crushed amaretti cookies. In small bowl, mix coffee flavor liqueur and remaining amaretti cookies; press mixture on bottom of 4 dessert bowls.

3. Spoon softened chocolate ice cream over cookie mixture. Garnish with whipped cream and reserved amaretti. Freeze until ready to serve. Makes 4 servings.

CHOCOLATE TORTE

A perfect make ahead frozen dessert. Very fancy, too.

3 egg whites
½ tsp. cream of tartar
¾ c. sugar
¾ c. finely ground pecans
2 c. heavy cream

¾ c. chocolate syrup
1 tsp. vanilla
Chocolate curls for garnish
  (optional)
Pecan halves for garnish (optional)

Cover 2 baking sheets with aluminum foil. Draw 8 inch circle in center on each sheet, using layer cake pan as guide. Beat egg whites with cream of tartar in large bowl with mixer until foamy. Beat in sugar with mixer at high speed, 1 tablespoon at a time; beat 2 to 3 minutes after all sugar is incorporated until stiff and glossy. Fold in pecans. Divide meringue equally onto circles; spread evenly, smoothing tops and edges.

Bake in preheated very slow oven (275°) for 45 minutes. (Bake as close to center of oven as possible and midway through baking, reverse position of baking sheets, both horizontally and front to back.) After 45 minutes baking time, turn off oven but leave meringues in oven with door closed 45 minutes longer. Cool baking sheets on wire rack to room temperature.

Beat cream in medium size bowl until very stiff. Fold in syrup and vanilla. Gently loosen meringues from foil with long thin blade spatula. If meringues stick in spots, simply dip spatula briefly in hot water. Place a meringue, right side up, on serving platter. Spread with half the chocolate cream, pushing it right to edge. Top with second meringue, pushing down lightly to anchor. Top with remaining chocolate cream, swirling into hills and valleys. Freeze 6 hours.

To serve, let torte stand on counter 15 to 20 minutes until slightly softened. Garnish with chocolate curls and pecan halves, if you wish. Serves 10 to 12.

CHOCOLATE TORTONI

A delicious chocolate dessert, and so fancy.

1 c. amaretti cookie crumbs
2 Tbsp. melted butter
2 (1 oz.) sq. unsweetened chocolate
  bits
1 (6 oz.) pkg. semi-sweet chocolate
  bits
4 egg whites

⅛ tsp. cream of tartar
⅛ tsp. salt
¼ c. sugar
2 c. heavy cream
2 tsp. sugar
1 tsp. vanilla
½ c. toasted chopped almonds

Garnish:

Whipped cream
Whole toasted almonds, dipped in
  semi-sweet chocolate

Strawberries

Combine cookie crumbs and melted butter in small bowl; blend well. Firmly press mixture in even layer over bottom of 8 inch springform pan. Chill while preparing tortoni mixture.

Melt unsweetened chocolate in top of double boiler over' hot, not boiling, water. In a separate double boiler, melt semi-sweet chocolate bits over hot, but not boiling water.

Beat egg whites with cream of tartar and salt in small bowl until foamy. Gradually beat in the ¼ cup sugar, 1 tablespoon at a time, until soft peaks form.

Beat the 2 cups heavy cream in large bowl until stiff. Beat in the 2 teaspoons sugar, vanilla, and melted unsweetened chocolate; blend well.

Fold the beaten egg whites, toasted almonds, and melted semi-sweet chocolate into the whipped cream mixture until no streaks of white remain; there may be some small chunks of chocolate.

Turn into prepared pan. Smooth top with rubber spatula. Cover pan with aluminum foil. Freeze until firm or for up to 3 days.

To serve, remove side of pan. Garnish with whipped cream, almonds, strawberries, and chocolate leaves, if you wish. Serves 12.

MINT-CHOCOLATE CHIP ICE CREAM

A hint of mint makes this ice cream extra special.

1 egg
⅓ c. sugar
¾ c. milk
¾ c. heavy (whipping) cream
1 tsp. vanilla extract
¼ tsp. mint extract
¼ c. semi-sweet mini chocolate chips
Few drops green food color (optional)

With electric mixer, beat egg and sugar until thick and cream color. Add milk, cream, vanilla and mint extract, chocolate chips, and food color. Mix well and pour into ice cream maker. Freeze to desired consistency. This may be eaten immediately or kept frozen. Makes 1 pint.

Notes

BEVERAGES

HOMEMADE IRISH CREAM LIQUEUR

Just divinely delicious and so easy to make.

1¾ c. of your favorite liquor (Irish whiskey, brandy, rum, bourbon, Scotch or rye whiskey)
1 (14 oz.) can sweetened condensed milk (not evaporated milk)

1 c. (½ pt.) whipping or light cream
4 eggs
2 Tbsp. chocolate flavored syrup
2 tsp. instant coffee
1 tsp. vanilla
½ tsp. almond extract

In blender container, combine all ingredients; blend until smooth. Serve over ice if desired. Store tightly covered in refrigerator up to one month. Stir before serving. Makes about 5 cups.

OLD-FASHIONED HOT CHOCOLATE

Wonderful to serve on a cold day.

1 oz. sq. unsweetened chocolate
⅓ c. boiling water
1 qt. milk, scalded
⅓ c. sugar

Pinch of salt
½ tsp. vanilla
Marshmallows or whipped cream (optional)

Place chocolate in top of double boiler; bring water to a boil. Reduce heat to low; cook until chocolate melts. Gradually add 1⅓ cups boiling water, stirring constantly. Remove from heat; set aside.

Combine scalded milk, sugar, and salt in a saucepan; add chocolate mixture, stirring well. Cook over low heat, stirring occasionally. Remove from heat; stir in vanilla. If desired, top with marshmallows or whipped cream. Makes 6 cups.

CHOCOLATE COFFEE

Serve this chocolate coffee for a quick chocolate treat.

Try a "Kiss in a cup." Before you pour your coffee, put in a milk chocolate Kiss for a luscious treat. Serves 1.

CAPPUCCINO

Yes, you can prepare it at home with no special equipment - and with all the delicious flavor!

¾ c. instant espresso coffee powder
1 sq. unsweetened chocolate, chopped
Sugar

4 c. milk
1 c. heavy or whipping cream
½ tsp. vanilla
Ground cinnamon (optional)

About 30 minutes before serving: In 4 quart saucepan over high heat, heat instant espresso, chocolate, 4 cups water, and 3 tablespoons sugar until chocolate melts, sugar dissolves, and mixture boils, stirring occasionally. Add milk; cook over medium heat until tiny bubbles form around edge and mixture is hot, stirring occasionally.

Meanwhile, in small bowl, with mixer at medium speed, beat heavy or whipping cream, vanilla, and 1 tablespoon sugar until soft peaks form. To serve, with wire whisk, beat hot espresso mixture until foamy; pour into cups. Top each serving of Cappuccino with dollop of whipped cream. If you like, sprinkle with cinnamon. Makes 8 cups or 12 servings.

COFFEE PUNCH

A fast delicious party punch.

2 qt. strong coffee
2 c. milk
½ c. sugar
1 tsp. vanilla

1 c. whipping cream
1 c. dark rum
1 qt. chocolate ice cream
Miniature marshmallows (optional)

Combine coffee, milk, sugar, and vanilla; stir until sugar dissolves. Chill until ready to serve.

Just before serving, stir whipping cream and rum into coffee mixture. Scoop ice cream into a punch bowl; gradually pour coffee mixture over ice cream. Float marshmallows on top if desired. Makes about 1 gallon.

HOT CHOCOLATE

Combine rum and chocolate for a delicious beverage.

Pour 1 generous jigger of light or dark rum into a cup of hot chocolate. Whipped cream optional. Serves 1.

HOT MOCHA

Liquor can be added and the recipe doubled for a party punch.

¼ c. decaffeinated freeze dried
   coffee
½ c. chocolate syrup

4½ c. milk, scalded
¾ c. whipped sweetened cream

Measure coffee and syrup into a carafe or pitcher. Stir in scalded milk and stir until coffee is dissolved. Pour into cups or mugs. Top with whipped cream and garnish with grated chocolate if desired. Makes about 5 cups or 6 servings.

FAVORITE HOT CHOCOLATE

Very rich! Just delicious!

1½ c. sugar
½ c. cocoa
¾ tsp. salt
5 c. water

1 (13 oz.) can evaporated milk
2 c. milk
Marshmallows (optional)

Combine sugar, cocoa, and salt in a large Dutch oven; mix well. Slowly stir in water; bring to a boil. Add milk; cook until thoroughly heated.

Place marshmallows in individual cups if desired; fill cups with hot chocolate. Makes 2½ quarts.

COCOA-COFFEE

Instant coffee and cocoa are combined to make this delicious drink.

1 c. instant cocoa mix
⅓ c. instant coffee granules

4 c. boiling water
Whipped cream

Combine cocoa mix, instant coffee, and boiling water; stir until coffee granules dissolve. Garnish each serving with whipped cream. Makes 1 quart.

Notes

INDEX OF RECIPES

FANCY FROZEN DESSERTS, ICE CREAMS, AND THEIR SAUCES

BEVERAGES